SELLING TO

BIG

COMPANIES

SELLING TO
BIG
COMPANIES

JILL KONRATH

KAPLAN PUBLISHING

Vice President and Publisher: Cynthia A. Zigmund
Senior Acquisitions Editor: Michael Cunningham
Development Editor: Karen Murphy
Project Editor: Caitlin Ostrow
Interior Design: Lucy Jenkins
Cover Design: Michael Warrell, Design Solutions
Typesetting: Todd Bowman

Published by Kaplan Publishing,
a division of Kaplan, Inc.

Library of Congress Cataloging-in-Publication Data

Konrath, Jill.
  Selling to big companies / Jill Konrath.
     p. cm.
  Includes index.
  ISBN 1-4195-1562-4
  1. Selling. I. Title.
  HF5438.25.K66 2005
  658.8'1–dc22
                                        2005015092

For information about ordering Kaplan Publishing books at special quantity discounts, please call 1-800-KAP-ITEM or write to Kaplan Publishing, 888 Seventh Avenue, 22nd floor, New York, NY 10106.

DEDICATION

To Fred, Katie, and Ryan, whose love and support made all this possible.

DEDICATION

Contents

PART TWO
BUILD THE FOUNDATION

PART THREE
LAUNCH THE CAMPAIGN

Writing this book took only a few months, but it's taken a lifetime of experience to make it worth reading.

I am grateful to Xerox Corporation for hiring me into this wonderful profession and giving me a solid foundation for sales success. While there, I worked with some of the best sales professionals in the entire world: Mary Kath, Tom Lowe, Bonnie Guski, Bruce Malmgren, and many more. Thanks for your friendship and for setting a benchmark of excellence that stays with me today. A special thanks goes to Diane Gulbrandson, my first sales manager, who believed in me long before I had confidence in my own abilities.

To all my clients over the past 15 years, thank you for the many opportunities to work with your fine sales organizations. The projects we worked on together enabled me to both broaden and deepen my expertise. I wouldn't be where I am today without you. Thanks especially to Bob Cummins, John Wadie, Barb Cederberg, Ken Bozevich, Hans Koppen, Nancy Harrower, Bill Goodwin, Joe Weaver, Bill Markwardt, Greg Arnold, Michael Springer, Bob Decker, and John Fitzgerald.

To the thousands of people around the world who read my e-zine: Thanks for letting me know that my writing makes a difference. I am humbled by your kind e-mails and feel a deep sense of responsibility to keep giving you quality material to help in your sales efforts.

Thanks to my younger colleagues, Andrew Ralston and Brian Carroll, who have dragged me kicking and screaming into the online world. Because of your support, my peers now think I'm an expert on leveraging the Internet to drive business growth.

A special thanks to the many women in my life who keep challenging me to grow beyond my comfort zone. My Awesome Women colleagues, Faith Ralston, Nancy Stephan, Rita Webster, and Marci Heerman, have supported me through thick and thin. They've helped me find my voice, fine-tune my message, and create my future.

Many thanks also to Joan Autrey, Diane Matalamaki, Mary Kaase, Betsy Buckley, and Lynn Vannelli. You've been great friends and cheerleaders as I move through the stages of my life. Ardath Albee, thanks for providing feedback on the material in the book in real time. Kristin Kowler, I value your deep insights into how to simplify and integrate my message.

Thank you to all those people who helped me turn this book into a reality. Michael Nick, I appreciate your connections. John Willig, thanks for being my agent and handling all the tough stuff. Michael Cunningham and the staff at Dearborn Trade Publishing, thanks for believing in this book as much as I did. You've done a super job!

And last, but certainly not least, thank you to my husband Fred and two children, Katie and Ryan, for all the patience you showed while I wrote this book. I am forever grateful that you are in my life.

Several years ago my sales training business came to a screeching halt. Within a several month period, I lost 95 percent of my work when my two biggest clients put a moratorium on all outside consulting. Because I was working with multiple divisions of these corporate giants, I thought I was safe. Unfortunately, when Wall Street started putting pressure on them to deliver better results, they made across-the-board cuts.

Contracts stopped midstream. Instead of having the next five months fully booked, I had nothing on my plate—and I mean nothing. Yet I found it impossible to pick up the phone and make sales calls.

Why? For the previous ten years, my business had grown with virtually no effort on my part. By doing a good job, one project quickly led to a second and a third. My name was passed on (with glowing praise) to different divisions and business units. When I met with prospective buyers, they were ready to start working. Over time, as I became an invaluable resource for my clients, they asked me to help in areas outside my expertise. Initially I declined, but before long I was leading strategy sessions, doing future scenario planning, and working in market development. All this was a big stretch from helping companies shorten time-to-revenue on new product launches. I loved it! It challenged me beyond my wildest dreams.

But it also wreaked havoc on my value proposition. If someone asked me what I did, I could go on for days about everything I was capable of doing for marketing and sales. As a sales trainer, I knew I needed a strong value proposition to capture the attention of corporate decision makers. Mine was so all over the map that I couldn't make calls. After over a decade of running a successful training firm, I was back at ground zero again trying to determine the direction of my company.

During that same time period, I did a pro bono project for a small magazine that catered to small and emerging businesses. Captivated by their impact on the economy, I spent hours online learning as much as

I could about the entrepreneurial market sector. I was stunned to discover that 75 percent of small businesses shut their doors because the owner was working too darn hard for the amount of money coming in.

For someone with my background, it was clear that they had a severe sales and marketing problem. I researched the available resources for these small firms that wanted to sell their products, services, and solutions to the corporate market and was appalled at how bad they were. I wanted to help, but I had no idea how I could impact these widely dispersed, cash-poor businesses.

One day it hit me: I'd create an online resource for these firms called SellingtoBigCompanies.com. On this site, they'd have access to the same quality information and training that was currently available only to large corporations. For almost a year, I poured my heart and soul into creating this resource for entrepreneurs, salespeople, independent professionals, and consultants.

During that time I did minimal consulting work and burned through nearly all my cash reserves. When the Web site was up and running, I was finally ready to return to my sales training business with renewed vigor and a full complement of new service offerings. I targeted companies I wanted to work for, found out who to contact, and started "dialing for dollars." I fully expected to land a few good clients in no time flat—just like I had in the past.

Boy, was I in for a shock! I couldn't reach a living soul. No one answered the phones anymore. All my calls rolled directly into voice mail. I agonized over leaving messages—should I or shouldn't I? It didn't seem to matter either way because no one called me back.

I was stymied. I'd never experienced problems getting in before. For someone who prided herself on her sales skills, it was incredibly humbling. At first I thought it might just be me—that maybe I was over the hill and no one wanted to talk with me anymore. But after checking around, I discovered other sellers were facing the same problem.

The struggle to get in was reaching epidemic proportions. Every person I talked with was having major difficulty setting up appointments with corporate buyers. It didn't seem to matter if they worked for a major corporation with huge name recognition or if they were a small one-person consulting firm. Sales approaches that had worked for years were no longer effective. In fact, they actually created more obstacles.

Sellers were scratching their heads wondering what to do next. If they couldn't get in, there was no way they could sell anything. I knew exactly how they felt. My bank account was running low, and I needed business.

Fortunately I love difficult sales problems, which is exactly what I was faced with. I challenged myself to figure out what it took to get into big companies again. I interviewed numerous people. I experimented with multiple techniques and strategies. I sharpened and fine-tuned the approaches that held promise. Then I focused on eliminating the obstacles I encountered along the way.

Lo and behold, I finally started getting appointments with key decision makers. I kept at it until I knew the process worked for anyone in business-to-business sales, regardless of their specific market focus. Since that time, nearly all my speaking and training has focused on what it takes to get into big companies. It's a huge issue that affects sellers across every industry. They don't have a clue what to do differently—which is why I wrote this book.

SELLING TO BIG COMPANIES OVERVIEW

It's a whole new world out there right now. New approaches are required for success in today's crazy marketplace. Doing more of the same old thing won't get you anywhere—and especially not into a large corporation. *Selling to Big Companies* shows you what it takes to get the attention of corporate decision makers today.

Part I: Accept the Challenge

In Part I you'll learn more about what's happening in the corporate world today that's causing you all these sales difficulties. You'll be introduced to:

- marketplace trends impacting your sales today, as well as your own self-defeating behaviors;
- how to break large corporations and your offering into bite-sized chunks so you can get your foot in the door;

- the world of the corporate decision maker and how to best break through their wall of resistance; and
- the new sales paradigm where you become the major differentiator.

Part II: Build the Foundation

This section of the book covers those key elements you need to have in place to move forward in today's sales environment. You'll learn how to:

- target the big companies where you have a high likelihood of sales success;
- evaluate your current value proposition to determine its effectiveness;
- strengthen your value proposition so it's highly appealing to corporate buyers;
- research big companies and uncover critical information that can help you advance your sales efforts; and
- leverage existing relationships and create new connections that can help you get in.

Part III: Launch the Campaign

In this segment of the book, you'll discover how to integrate what you've learned about your value proposition and targeted prospects to:

- identify who makes decisions for your product or service within the big companies;
- craft a multitouch account entry campaign that breaks through all the marketing clutter;
- create and deliver enticing voice mail messages that attract the attention of corporate decision makers; and
- develop customer-attracting letters and e-mails that stand out from the crowd and incite a positive response.

Part IV: Break Through the Barriers

This portion of the book focuses on overcoming the typical challenges you encounter in your attempts to get into big companies. You'll find out how to:

- engage in a business-oriented phone discussion with prospective customers;
- overcome common objections and obstacles to getting your foot in the door;
- turn gatekeepers into gate openers without the use of manipulative techniques; and
- keep your account entry campaign alive without sounding like you're desperate—even if you are.

Part V: Advance the Sale

The final section of this book is focused on when you actually meet with your prospect. Specifically, you'll discover how to:

- plan and implement a highly effective initial client meeting;
- converse with corporate decision makers regarding their critical business issues;
- advance the sales process to its logical next step—with ease; and
- turn yourself into a competitive advantage!

HOW TO USE THIS BOOK

Selling to Big Companies was written to be an ongoing resource for your sales efforts. Because so much has changed in the past few years, I recommend that you read it through at least once to get a sense of today's sales environment and what it takes to be successful. Because many of the concepts in this book build upon each other, it's important to read them in order too.

After the first reading, I strongly suggest a focus on your value proposition. If you can't clearly articulate the business results that customers realize from using your product, service, or solution, then the rest of the book is a moot point. Weak value propositions are the most common root cause of ineffective selling.

Once you've nailed down your value proposition, then work on developing your campaign. It doesn't matter what you tackle first—voice mails, direct mail, or e-mail account entry strategies. Start in the medium you are most comfortable with and then work on refining your approach. This book is full of guidance on what you need to do to build your momentum.

The Account Entry Tool Kit in Appendix A will help you better implement the concepts and ideas presented in the book. Also, you'll find a variety of resources you can use to increase your sales effectiveness.

I wrote *Selling to Big Companies* to help you get your foot in the door of large corporate accounts and win big contracts. May it provide you with all the insights you need to achieve your goals. Have a great year selling!

Part One

ACCEPT
THE CHALLENGE

1

WHY NOBODY CALLS YOU BACK

Selling to big companies is tough. Really tough. It seems as if those big corporations have erected huge impenetrable fortresses around their offices just to keep you out. Decision makers' names are shrouded in secrecy. Phone calls are nearly always routed to voice mail. It's next to impossible to talk to a real live human being. And don't hold your breath if you're waiting for someone to call you back!

Yet, if you're like most people, you look at those big companies and think, "If only I could get my foot in the door." Visions of large contracts or sizable commission checks swirl through your head. You'd give anything for a few long-term corporate relationships with a highly profitable and consistent revenue stream.

Besides that, having prestigious firms like P&G, BP, or 3M as customers would be proof positive to other prospective buyers that your sales offering is world class. Deep inside, you know their stamp of approval would simplify your other sales efforts.

But how do you get into these big companies? What does it take to get a meeting with a decision maker? How do you get in if you don't know even one single person who works there? Or, if you're not quite ready to tackle these corporate behemoths, how do you penetrate firms larger than you're working with today?

THE OVERWHELMING
CORPORATE MYSTIQUE

The very thought of working with big accounts is often overwhelming for many sellers. Even the most accomplished professionals become tongue tied when they think about contacting a corporate bigwig. Besieged by self-doubt, they question if they could possibly bring any value to a business relationship with a big company. They stress over how to handle pricing issues or competitive objections. They obsess over how to avoid sounding stupid to those bright, talented people who work for big companies.

I know because I've had all these feelings myself. When I first started selling, I worked a geographic territory for Xerox that excluded the large corporations. For three years, I had exceptional success selling copiers to small-sized and medium-sized businesses.

When I finally got promoted, I was terrified. I imagined my new decision makers to be imbued with superhuman qualities. In my mind, they were savvy businesspeople with no time for peons like me who were just learning the ropes. It didn't help matters either when one of the top sales representatives in my firm said to me, "Now you're playing with the Big Boys, Jill. We'll see how good you really are."

It took me a long time to realize that decision makers in big companies were normal human beings. They just happened to work for a large firm.

I had to relearn this lesson five years later when I started my sales training business. For some strange reason, I assumed that big corporations employed their own top-notch sales trainers whose skills far surpassed mine. It took me a while before I realized that they didn't have all the answers. My expertise complemented and extended their existing sales training capabilities.

In order to find that out, though, I had to meet with corporate decision makers. I needed to discover that their programs did not address all their sales training needs. That's where we come smack dab back to the questions that haunt everyone who sells to big companies: Who do

I see? And, what do I say when I get there? These selling challenges are even more complicated today because it's so difficult to get face-to-face meetings with prospective buyers.

SAIL INTO THE "PERFECT STORM"

If you've being trying to get into big companies, you know just how tough it is. The truth is that it's only going to get harder in the future. What you're facing now is a situation caused by the convergence of multiple market factors that have, in effect, created a "perfect storm" for sellers.

What's happening in the business community that's making it so hard to sell today? These are the current trends impacting your sales efforts:

- Big companies keep getting bigger and more global. They're constantly restructuring, reorganizing, and rightsizing. This continuous state of flux leads to an overworked, stressed-out workforce with a strong aversion to any more change.
- Corporate decision makers continue to embrace technology in order to enhance communications, educate themselves, protect their time, and prevent interruptions in their already overcrowded schedule.
- Competition gets tougher all the time as copycat products and services pop up virtually overnight. Prospects don't believe any company can maintain its competitive edge for long.
- Bombarded by a daily onslaught of marketing, corporate buyers are increasingly immune to even the slightest hint of self-promoting puffery by salespeople. This storm isn't going to blow over any time soon either.

These trends will make it even more difficult for you to:

- figure out where decisions are being made and who is actually involved in the decision process;
- entice stressed-out customers to take time from their busy schedules to meet with you;
- differentiate your offering from competitors without destroying your profit margins; and

- bring exceptional value to client meetings—so much so that decision makers will want to work with you despite higher pricing.

To be successful in this rapidly and radically changing sales environment, it's imperative to rethink your account entry strategy. Your first job is to examine your current approach to big companies to determine where changes are needed.

STOP SOUNDING LIKE A SELF-SERVING SALESPERSON

Let's take a look at what you might do today to set up an appointment with a corporate decision maker. If you're like many sellers, just the thought of picking up that phone to call strangers turns your stomach. All you can think about are those disgusting telemarketers who interrupt your evening meal and read from a canned script. Words like sleazy, slimy, and manipulative pop into your mind. Vowing to be different, you agonize over what you're going to say so you don't sound so "cheesy."

As a seller, you most likely would rather go to the dentist for a root canal than make those dreaded prospecting calls. Inside, a little voice in your head keeps saying: "Why bother—no one ever answers."

When you can't put it off any longer, you finally make the call. Sure enough, your prospect's voice mail kicks in, "Hi. This is Terry. Please leave a message and I'll call you back as soon as I can."

Frustrated by another fruitless attempt to reach this decision maker, you decide to leave a message this time. You quickly sit up straight in your chair, smile, and muster up all the enthusiasm you possibly can as you say,

"Mr. Hope. This is Jane Manthey. I'm with Generic Strategies, a leading design services firm in this area. We offer a wide range of marketing communications and consulting services. In fact, we pride ourselves on offering our customers one-stop shopping for all their design needs. We recently introduced some exciting new state-of-the-art services that earned us the highest recognition from Krumstock Research.

"I'd love to set up a time to find out a bit more about your needs in this area and tell you more about these new services we're so excited about. Please give me a call at your earliest convenience. My number is . . . I look forward to meeting with you."

Hanging up the phone, you sigh in relief. Another call done. Over with. Truth be told, you're rather pleased with your performance. Your message was gracious. You weren't pushy—just informative. You demonstrated enough passion for your offering without going overboard. All in all, your call was very professional, if you don't say so yourself.

Sound familiar? Well, if you left a message that was even close to the one above, you sounded exactly like every other salesperson trying to reach this decision maker. He or she probably has numerous other identical messages in his or her voice mail every single day.

While most sellers agonize over how to best describe their company and offering, they rarely stop to listen to what they say from their prospect's point of view.

Take a moment to imagine yourself as a busy decision maker listening to the above message. Would you be interested in meeting with the caller? What would you get out of that meeting? Anything worth your time? The only people who gain from getting together at meetings like these are the sellers. They get a chance to tell clients about their services—whether they're of value to clients or not. That's self-serving sales behavior, and it doesn't work in today's environment. While I don't know any decision makers who would waste one second of their time with sellers who use this approach, it's the approach almost every seller uses.

CRACK THE CORPORATE CODE

Much as you might fantasize that your phone is ringing off the hook with corporate buyers who can't wait to learn about your offering, it's not going to happen using the "same old, same old" approach. Nor do these prospective customers cruise down the streets or enter local office buildings looking for signs that say Great Technology Services, Bob's Leadership Consulting, or Wonderful Widgets.

While you may be stymied by the barricades surrounding their offices, please realize that some sellers are getting in and being extremely successful. Their products or services aren't any better than yours. They don't offer better value or cheaper pricing. They don't have superior promotional activities, huge marketing budgets, or work for a company with a household name. They've just learned what it takes to crack the corporate code in order to land a meeting with key decision makers. You can do it too. There's no magic involved, just a lot of rethinking of what you're doing.

Most sellers think that what happens when they're actually talking to a prospective customer determines if they get the business or not. They're wrong.

Successful sellers today spend significantly more time thinking, analyzing, researching, and preparing for their client meetings than average sellers do. They're extremely "thought-full," and this singular quality is what determines the outcome of all their interactions with customers.

If your "message" to customers is perceived as self-serving, no one will want to meet with you. Successful selling starts from a solid, in-depth understanding of your customers. You have to think, feel, sense, and evaluate from their perspective in order to develop and implement an effective account entry strategy.

KEY POINTS

- It's tough to set up meetings with prospective buyers at major corporations; the difficulty you're experiencing is not in your imagination.
- It's not going to get any easier for you in the future. Multiple marketplace factors are converging to create a "perfect storm" for sellers.
- Corporate decision makers are normal people who just happen to work for a large company. They are not imbued with superhuman qualities.
- The traditional approach to setting up appointments makes you sound like a self-serving salesperson who is interested only in your own success.
- To break through the barriers erected by corporate buyers, you need to develop new account entry approaches today.

2

DOING BUSINESS WITH BIG(GER) COMPANIES

While everyone dreams of selling to big companies, the harsh reality is that fewer sellers are getting in today than ever before. If you don't have many large accounts in your customer base, it's easy to imbue them with larger-than-life attributes.

From the outside of a big company you may envision a workforce of the brightest, most talented, and most motivated people on this earth. You picture them working in a well-oiled, flawless system. You imagine seamless integration between business units, subsidiaries, divisions, and even departments.

Knowing they have deep pockets, you presume they must have the latest and greatest technology as well as the most innovative processes. You suspect they have world-class training, well-run meetings, and access to whatever resources they need.

If you make these grandiose assumptions about big companies, you'll be in for a big shock when you actually start working with them. In truth, everywhere you turn there is room for improvement. Large corporations constantly look to outside resources to help them get better. They need fresh perspectives to meet their challenges. They want to use products that provide them with the best possible value for their investment. Opportunity is rampant, just waiting to be capitalized on.

THE ECSTASY OF CORPORATE CLIENTS

Every large corporation has the potential to be a gold mine for you and your company. Perhaps the biggest upside is that once you get in, there are so many places you can go to sell your product or service. For example, if your first sale is to research and development (R&D) in one division, it's so much easier to get into similar areas of other divisions. If you land a contract with a specific business unit, the second and third contracts to this unit come so much faster. Once corporate clients trust your judgment, quality, reliability, and integrity, they will invite you to participate in discussions that give you an insider's view of their operations. After a while, you almost become a fixture in their companies because you're there so often working on various projects.

My very first contract in a large global firm was for $10,000. Eight years and $500,000+ later, I was still doing work for the organization. During that time, I worked with a multitude of divisions doing a wide variety of projects in my area of expertise. Some were extraordinarily challenging, enabling me to develop skills I didn't even know I had.

If you keep doing a good job, your business grows exponentially. Marketing and sales costs become virtually nonexistent as you move from project to project. In some respects, big companies are a lot less price sensitive than smaller businesses. They recognize that good people and products aren't cheap. Plus, they're not spending their own hard-earned dollars. They don't have to decide between feeding their kids or contracting with your company.

THE AGONY OF CORPORATE CLIENTS

Of course, there are downsides to working with big accounts as well. When their financial picture isn't looking rosy, the Wall Street analysts put the pressure on and suddenly everything comes to a grinding halt. Budgets are immediately frozen, and across-the-board cuts are commonplace. If you have too many eggs in one basket, your personal financial picture may become bleak overnight. The same thing happens with the arrival of a new management team. Everyone goes into a "hold mode" until they know what's happening.

Shifts in philosophy also put long-term relationships at risk. I recently spoke with a print broker who handled 90 percent of the printing needs of a large corporation. One day the executives decided to spread out the work to mitigate their risk. A huge chunk of his business disappeared overnight. The same thing happened to another seller I know whose business came to a screeching halt when her biggest customer decided to implement reverse auctions—a "how low will you go" online bidding contest for suppliers.

Sometimes big corporations get arrogant too. They know the prestige value of having them as a client and how much you need them to keep in business. When this happens, they make suppliers jump through hoops to work with them, even dictating what they're willing to pay for products or services.

Despite these drawbacks, the pluses of doing work with large accounts far outweigh the negatives. Because the sheer scope of available opportunities is immense, they drive you to take your business to the next level. They expect you to dig in and learn about their organization and their industry. They challenge you to tackle projects beyond your normal scope, knowledge, or experience level. Ultimately you develop a broader and deeper expertise that enhances your overall marketability. Finally, there's nothing that beats having well-known corporations on your customer list.

BREAK BIG COMPANIES INTO BITE-SIZED CHUNKS

Most sellers create their own mental showstoppers that prevent them from getting into big corporations. Pursuing business with these large organizations can be really overwhelming at first, especially if you've never worked for one. To reduce the intimidation factor, you will find it helps to break the big company down into smaller units that you can get your arms and mind around.

Let's take a look at General Electric (GE) to get a better feel of the actual components of a corporate monolith. GE is a huge global diversified technology, media, and financial services company. With annual revenues in excess of $150 billion, the organization operates in over 100 countries and employs over 300,000 people worldwide. Unless you're a huge corporation yourself, there's no way that you'll ever do business with all of GE.

When you start looking deeper, you'll see that GE is made up of six businesses: Commercial Financial Services, Industrial, Consumer Finance, Infrastructure, Healthcare, and NBC Universal. Each of these subsets of GE is its own multibillion-dollar business with thousands of employees, operations in multiple countries, and facilities across the world. The size and scope of these business units within a company can be downright overwhelming.

Let's say you decide to investigate GE Healthcare—a $14 billion unit with 40,000+ employees. Breaking this business unit down further, you'll discover that it's composed of many different divisions. You could pursue work with any of the various clinical specialty units such as cardiology, oncology, or surgery. Or you could decide to target one of their solution areas, such as Biosciences, Diagnostic Imaging, Information Technology, Clinical Systems, or Services. Because they're contacted by far fewer sellers, it's typically much easier to get into these subsets of GE Healthcare. Finally, each of these divisions can be broken down into functional areas or departments. Within each division, you'll find marketing, sales, R&D, manufacturing, services, legal, information technology, human resources, and more.

> The easiest and fastest way to get into a big company is through one of its functional areas.

Rather than being awestruck by the magnitude of a large corporation, break it down into bite-sized pieces that are more manageable for you to tackle. For many people, it's easiest to get in through a functional unit because they can:

- find the decision maker's name;
- conduct due diligence without being overwhelmed;
- figure out where the problems and gaps might be in their operation;
- determine the difference they can make; and
- implement a customized "getting in" strategy.

Breaking a big company into bite-sized parts is the best way to begin. It prevents you from becoming overwhelmed by the sheer complexity of the organization, enabling you to turn your dream into a reality.

EMPLOY A FOOT-IN-THE-DOOR
SALES STRATEGY

I believe in making it as easy as humanly possible to get your initial contract with big companies. The best way to do that is to find and fill an immediate and urgent need for your prospect. It doesn't necessarily mean a huge contract. In fact, you can get started in a very small way and leverage that one piece of business into a highly profitable, multi-year relationship.

Once you're in, you're in! Do good work for your client and build your relationship. Keep your eyes open for emerging needs, other problems requiring resolution, and gaps between your client's desired future and today's reality. More business will materialize if you keep your focus on helping your clients improve their operations.

Find Your Most Effective Focal Point

When pursuing corporate contracts, most sellers want to ensure that decision makers know all about the full range of products, services, or solutions that they provide. This lack of specificity is extraordinarily detrimental to their sales objective and actually creates massive roadblocks for them.

Years ago, I discovered that it was much easier to get into big companies if I focused my entire "getting in" strategy around one very specific business problem related to the success of the new product launches. Many companies do a terrible job of preparing their field sales organization to sell the new products or services they're introducing. As a result, sales revenue typically lags far behind projections. Because the marketing and sales teams blame each other for the dismal results, they never really solve the problem.

My targeted customers clearly had an immediate, urgent need for help. The success or failure of a new offering is highly visible in the company. If the new product flopped, everyone knew about it. Careers were at stake. Windows of opportunity would be lost, market share could erode, and the lifetime profitability of the product would be seriously diminished.

Not only that, but companies have a lot more money at launch time. So despite the fact that I was capable of doing training on a wide range of sales skills, I chose to focus my "getting in" strategy on helping salespeople be successful at launch.

In my early meetings with corporate decision makers, I never confused my message by sharing with them the entire breadth of my services. The focus of our discussion was always on their product launch issues. Once I had a successful project under my belt, I let my clients know how I could help them in other ways.

How can you uncover your own foot-in-the-door strategies? Here are a several ways you can tackle that challenge.

Let Your Customers Tell You

Look at your existing customers to see if there are any similarities in how you got your first contract with these accounts. Ask yourself:

- Did you start out tackling a specific type of problem or opportunity? If so, what was it?
- Did you have some unique product, capability, or service that interested the decision makers? If so, why was it of interest? What value did it provide?
- Did they choose your services because they didn't think their existing supplier could address some aspect of their business? If so, what were the gaps you filled?

One of my clients is a small company that's just gearing up for the big time. This firm has developed some software that makes it incredibly easy for companies to update their Web sites without the information technology (IT) department getting involved. Initially, the firm was willing to take on any project to fund its growth. Now, the management team is getting serious about taking the business to the next level.

In analyzing the company's past successes, it turns out that the best foot-in-the-door strategy also happens to be with product launches. One of its best clients started out as a $50,000 launch project and grew to over $500,000 in revenue in just a few years. From now on, the company will focus its marketing and sales efforts on product introductions despite the fact that the software could be used in a hundred different applications. It's a superb door opener for this firm.

Find the White Space

I strongly suggest taking a good hard look at your competitors too. Every single one has some weaknesses or limitations; no single company is great at everything. Look for the "missing links" in their offering and exploit them to get into the big company. Don't go head-to-head with existing competitors. Instead, find the gaps.

When I pursued new-product-launch opportunities, I never competed against any of the big training companies because the work was too customized. Nor did I compete with marketing communications firms because I created tools for salespeople, not customers.

A fairly large professional services client of mine is pursuing specific types of risk management projects now with large corporate giants. Why? Because the Big Four consulting firms are swamped with all the changes required by recent government legislation and can't handle these "less urgent" matters. Some day when the Big Four consultants wake up, they'll discover a formidable competitor in their accounts who has developed a strong toehold while their attention was focused elsewhere.

Take the Crumbs

When you're trying to get into a big company, be willing to take whatever project you can—even if it's not your favorite. My first project with a big division of a large corporation had nothing to do with my expertise. I helped create an internal document to "sell" their field sales organization on a new compensation program. The national sales manager was terrified of a potential uprising from the sales force when they saw the new compensation plan. It was his number one priority. Ultimately, this group turned into my best client for five years.

I know a printer who called on one big account for several years with no success. The decision maker was totally happy with the current supplier . . . until one day when the vendor missed a deadline. Suddenly the decision maker had an urgent problem and needed help. The printer who'd been positioning himself for this moment made miracles happen in his company to get the job done on time. The crumbs turned into a highly profitable relationship.

Make Big Decisions Smaller

If your product or service costs a lot of money, it's much harder to get the first contract with a big company. There are budgetary issues, sign-off hassles, tons of people involved, increased visibility, and a great deal of personal risk involved for the decision maker.

Recently I did a comprehensive yearlong project with a prestigious client. When we first started talking about what needed to be done, I could tell they were nervous about a number of things—the scope, the costs, and even if working with me was the right decision. Rather than proposing the whole enchilada at the onset, I broke it down into pieces. I recommended they just get approval for Phase I initially because of what we'd learn in working together. We could reevaluate Phase II when it was time. By making my proposal smaller, I got in faster. By the time Phase II rolled around, they trusted me and valued my work. My second proposal was accepted without question.

If it's at all possible with your offering, think about how you might create smaller decisions. The easier you can make it for your customers to get started using your product or service, the faster you'll get into the big company.

Don't let yourself be intimidated by big companies. Despite their immense size, they're really a bunch of small companies filled with people who are doing the best job they know how to do. They're not perfect by any means.

Start by pursuing business with a functional area within a division of a business unit. Try to figure out what part of your offering might be the best foot-in-the-door strategy. Think easy.

KEY POINTS

- Large corporations are constantly looking for outside resources that can bring them fresh perspectives and better value.
- Working with big companies can provide your firm with the potential for exponential growth. While landing the first contract may be tough, the second and third contracts can come virtually overnight.
- On the downside, losing a contract with a major account can be devastating to your business and financial picture.
- It's easier to get into big companies if you break them into smaller sections; pursue opportunities with functional areas or departments within divisions for the easiest account penetration.
- Figure out which portion of your own offering addresses your prospect's urgent and compelling needs and leverage that aspect to initially get your foot in the door.

3

UNDERSTAND CORPORATE DECISION MAKERS

Have you spent much time in big companies lately? So much has changed in the past several years as they struggle to compete in today's fast-paced, hypercompetitive global economy. Large corporations are under intense and constant pressure to deliver strong financial results to their shareholders. If they miss their quarterly projections, Wall Street will be unforgiving. Stock prices plummet, the cost of borrowing money escalates, and layoffs follow.

These days large corporations are in a continual state of realignment, rightsizing, and reengineering as they struggle to find the best way to organize for maximum speed and profitability. Mergers and acquisitions are commonplace as companies look for economies of scale, new technologies, and market domination.

To top it off, corporate workforces have been slashed to the bare bones. Outsourcing continues to grow as these big accounts focus on their core competencies. Each survivor has picked up the work that used to be done by two or three other employees.

Pursuing business with these big companies puts you in the midst of this pressure-cooker environment. That's why it's imperative to understand how that environment impacts corporate decision makers as well as your own sales efforts.

THE WORLD OF CORPORATE DECISION MAKERS

Nearly every conversation I have with someone who works for a big company includes talk about having too much work and not nearly enough time. Employees are stressed out and overwhelmed with the sheer volume of work that needs to be done.

Corporate decision makers often face unrelenting, ever-escalating, unrealistic expectations to do more, better, faster.

Friends who work for large corporations tell me that no matter how hard they work, they can't seem to get ahead of the game. New fires keep popping up everywhere as urgent matters distract them from focusing on the important. Despite putting in 60-hour weeks, they can't seem to catch up.

I recently talked to an executive from a manufacturing firm whose salespeople were really struggling because of changing customer demands. Quite frankly, the firm's salespeople lacked the skills needed for success in today's market. But his group was under such intense pressure to "bring in the numbers" that he couldn't pull his salespeople out of the field for the kind of training that would help them succeed. Because they didn't have time to address these problems, they were forced to work even harder all the while they were slipping further and further behind.

Busy, Busy, Busy

Technology has made it even more difficult for corporate decision makers to stay on top of their workload. Many of them get nearly 200 e-mails each day. Why? Certainly, e-mailing is easy to do. By copying in every Tom, Dick, and Harry, employees look like they're really working hard—a perception that fearful people want to maintain in a world of constant downsizing. Unfortunately, by keeping everyone "in the loop," they actually exacerbate their problems.

Last month, a marketing manager from a health care organization told me she had to get into the office at 6:30 AM each day just so she could stay caught up on her e-mails and voice mails. A few days later, I heard about a director from a pharmaceutical company who went into work at 4:30 AM daily so he had time to work without interruption.

Looking busy is important in an environment where you could lose your job. So is activity. Recently, the head of training for a large corporation told me that one of his direct reports bragged about having over 350 items on his "To Do" List. He felt that it demonstrated his importance and value to the organization. Clearly, he had much more to do than is humanly possible. Worse yet, nearly everything on his list was a top priority.

Turtles and Ostriches

Despite feeling like they're at the end of their rope, most corporate decision makers are amazingly silent when it comes to voicing their opinions about the current situation. Why? At a time when so many good people have been downsized, they don't want to be next. They prefer to remain quiet, doing as much as they can while maintaining the lowest profile possible. Often their focus is on pleasing their boss rather than dealing with the tough issues.

They're also risk averse when it comes to making decisions. Because of all the pressure on bottom-line results, nearly all expenditures must demonstrate a strong return on investment (ROI). Today many companies expect to achieve a payback in less than 12 months.

To mitigate their risk, corporate decision makers routinely involve many people in the decision process and hold meeting after meeting to ensure they make the right decision. Getting a contract signed sometimes takes forever; sellers often have to jump through hoops to prove their product or service is the best and safest option.

Bad Case of Original Cynicism

Corporate decision makers aren't just struggling with an immense workload. Every day they're bombarded with thousands of marketing messages coming at them from every direction—television, road signs, radio, online, reading, mail, voice mail, and more. No matter what they do, they can't escape.

The noise from these pervasive and intrusive marketing practices has become unbearable to your prospective customers. They ignore unsolicited attempts to capture their attention. They disregard claims of superiority or differentiation, viewing those claims as marketing puffery created for the sole purpose of manipulation.

Corporate buyers are also incredibly savvy regarding their options. They know that products or services like yours are available everywhere—and probably at a lower cost. From their perspective, almost everything is a commodity. Cynicism reigns supreme. The only thing that seems to counteract it is real customer stories with actual, tangible, and measurable results.

THEY HAVEN'T GOT TIME FOR THE PAIN

The reality of the situation is that people in big companies really do have an unrealistic workload. Corporate decision makers are often too busy to:

- explore ways to improve their current systems, processes, and methodologies despite the fact that they may be losing an incredible amount of time and money;
- deal with the problems that haven't yet reached the crisis stage;
- plan proactively for their future;
- identify critical success factors;
- determine gaps in their operations; and
- implement much-needed strategies.

They get sucked into a chain of band-aid solutions, making knee-jerk decisions to put out the fires and jerry-rigging systems to keep them afloat. Rather than addressing root causes, they treat the symptoms, which ultimately leads to a whole slew of unintended negative consequences.

It's not that they don't care. Most people who work in a big company are good human beings who truly want to make a difference. They just have so much on their plate that they can't add one more thing—no matter how worthwhile it seems. After several years of working in an environment dictated by quarterly earnings and short-term thinking, they're operating in survival mode.

KNOW YOUR BIGGEST COMPETITORS

If you ask most sellers who their competitors are, you'll likely hear about other companies that offer products or services similar to theirs. In the traditional sense, that's true. If someone needs a copier, they evaluate Xerox, Canon, or Savin. If they need help with team building, they can work with a large management consulting firm or a small one-person business. But in today's marketplace, that's not where your biggest competition is coming from.

Long Live the Status Quo

The last thing in the world that corporate decision makers want is to create more work for themselves. They're already on overload, with a pile of work that just keeps growing. Even the very best, most positive change is disruptive.

For example, I limped along on my old computer for an eternity because I was so swamped with work. I knew that a new system would make a huge difference in my efficiency, but I also realized that it took time to get a new system set up right and to learn new ways of doing things. So I lived with the status quo until I had no choice but to abandon it.

Corporate decision makers are in exactly the same boat. With time as their most precious commodity, they don't seek out change. Even making a decision requires time to assess current processes, analyze the financial returns, evaluate options, negotiate contracts, set up a new vendor, and implement new ways of working. Just the thought of having to do all that extra work is exhausting.

Their extreme need to protect their time at all costs makes the status quo your most formidable competitor when selling to big companies. Change really has to be worthwhile to get someone to move.

Alternate Uses of Corporate Funds

As the old saying goes, "the squeaky wheel gets the grease." If decision makers can get by without making a change, they will. But ultimately something blows up in their face. Suddenly everyone's attention is diverted to this catastrophic occurrence, and money is poured into a solution. Even if no funding was allocated, it's siphoned off from other budgeted expenses.

Sometimes money is reallocated for other reasons too. Highly effective salespeople who help their customers understand the total costs of their current processes will always find funding available. Strong internal advocates for change can also influence where the budgeted money is spent.

In today's marketplace, you may really be up against a traditional competitor in a small percentage of the decisions being made. However, you're always fighting the status quo and other uses of corporate moneys.

MISTAKES YOU DON'T WANT TO MAKE

Now that you know about the corporate environment your prospective customers live in, let's take a look what that means in terms of mistakes to avoid.

Don't Waste Their Time

Corporate decision makers are extremely protective of their time. Because they're under constant pressure to deliver results, they zealously guard their schedule from interruptions of any sort. That's why they don't answer the phone or return phone calls—even though they know it's rude. They're terrified that you'll try to usurp one of their rare free moments.

Clearly, when you're dealing with these already overburdened people, not wasting their time needs to be topmost on your mind. When you contact them to set up an appointment, make sure to give them high-value reasons to meet with you.

Every single meeting with corporate buyers needs to provide value to them. Meandering conversations with no apparent purpose are killers. Your objective needs to be clear. Roles and responsibilities must be clearly defined. Questions need to be planned. Anything you can do to assure them that meeting with you in person or on the phone is a good investment of their time is well worth your effort.

Don't Try to Be Their Friend

Many old-time sales gurus will tell you how important it is to develop a personal relationship up front because "people buy from people they like." They recommend spending time getting to know your prospects, learning about their likes or dislikes, and finding out about their career goals, hobbies, and family life. They suggest that when you get to their office you look around for items to talk about, such as fishing trophies or pictures of their children.

This won't work today. Time-starved decision makers don't want to spend their precious time talking about a recent trip to Mexico with a stranger who's trying to sell them something.

In today's sales environment, you need to prove your business value first. For someone like me who really enjoys talking to people, this was a jolt to my system. In order to get my needs for "humanizing" the relationship met, I had to first focus on my prospect's needs for ensuring time is well spent. Show your value, demonstrate your worth, and make a difference. Then these decision makers want to have you as a friend.

Don't Expect Them to Tell You about Their Business

Again, this is a time-related issue, compounded by the ready access everyone has to information about their company. Corporate decision makers expect you to get yourself fully grounded about their business, industry, market trends, objectives, customers, competitors, and challenges—prior to initiating contact.

The reality, unfortunately, is that you can only learn so much when you're on the outside. They know that. As long as you do your homework and research their company before you call or meet with them, they're okay. But you'll totally destroy any credibility if you don't do that. Corporate decision makers won't take time to educate you in more depth about their firm until you've proven your willingness to invest your own time first.

Don't Give Them a Product Dump

Lots of sellers make this "dump" mistake. After trying for so long to get into the big company, they want to maximize every nanosecond of their time with the corporate buyer. Mistakenly, they believe that the best thing they can do is to explain their offering in excruciating detail.

Many times prospective decision makers will set this trap too by asking for information on your new products, services, solutions, or technology. Remember, they don't want to make a change unless they absolutely have to. Most are simply asking about it so they can find a reason to say "no" to you. Don't confuse this request for information with interest.

So don't focus on your offering, reciting its every feature and capability. This is the wrong place to put your emphasis. Absolutely no good comes from it.

Don't Use Any Self-Serving Verbiage

There's no better way to make yourself look like a cheesy salesperson than to describe your product or service with overstated qualifiers and adjectives. The more you proclaim that your offering is "absolutely the best," the less your prospect believes what you say.

They expect you to brag, hype, flaunt, and plug your wares or services. After all, that's how peddlers manipulate people into buying their goods at the highest price possible. Because peddlers can't be trusted, don't peddle! You hate doing it, and they hate hearing it.

Don't Expect Them to Intuit the Value of Your Offering

This may be a blinding flash of the obvious, but really, really busy people don't have time to think. Nor do they have time to translate what they hear into quantifiable metrics that are meaningful to their organization.

Telling a prospect that your solution improves services is worthless. So is that fact that it's made of certain materials, utilizes the most up-to-date technology, or helps prevent employee turnover. You may think that it isn't necessary to spell out the true value of your offering because customers "know" what it means.

Perhaps they do understand that value at some level. But they don't have time to analyze its impact on their own operations. They're too busy putting out those fires. They don't know how much money is seeping or even gushing from their bottom line because of their current processes. If they did, they'd have acted already. Never, ever expect corporate decision makers to intuit the value of your offering or make the calculations themselves.

People who work in big companies today are under intense pressure and stretched to the max. Certainly this creates challenges for you when you're trying to get your foot in the door. It also creates opportunities for the savvy seller, and that's what we'll look at in the next chapter.

KEY POINTS

- Corporate decision makers are under extreme pressure to deliver ever-escalating results faster, but with fewer resources and at less cost.
- Your biggest competition today is the status quo. Unnecessary change only adds to the stress of an already overburdened workforce.
- Sales pitches or sales presentations are totally ineffective. The last thing decision makers want to do is spend their precious time listening to a talking brochure.
- To be heard in today's crazy sales environment, shout the business value of your offering loudly and clearly. Don't expect your prospects to infer it; they're much too busy for that.
- Never, ever waste your prospect's time. Make sure every conversation or meeting is well-planned and provides high value.

4

IT'S ALL ABOUT MAKING A DIFFERENCE

Despite all the apparent obstacles to getting your foot in the door of big companies, it truly can be the best of times to pursue opportunities with them. But it's certainly not business as usual. What worked a few years ago is no longer effective for selling into the corporate market. New ways of thinking and acting are now required for sales success.

You likely have some preconceived notions about what it takes to be good at sales. Over the years I've talked to so many people who feel woefully deficient in this role because they:

- aren't glib conversationalists;
- hate "pitching" their product;
- detest "bragging" about their capabilities;
- don't "wing it" well; and
- lack strong closing skills.

If that list describes your thinking, then you're in luck because those so-called "skills" are the kiss of death in today's sales environment. Chatterboxes waste the busy decision maker's time. Sellers with perfected "pitches" come across as cardboard characters interested only in their personal gains. Those who "wing it" discover that their prospects no longer want to meet with them. Great closers create obstacle after obstacle, effectively derailing their own sales efforts.

THE NEW MODEL FOR SALES SUCCESS

Sales is not a bunch of mysterious, manipulative techniques you can master that trick customers into buying from you. We're not talking about selling snake oil and getting quickly out of town. We're talking about establishing long-term, mutually beneficial relationships.

The old way of selling is dead, dead, dead. As the table below shows, sellers who follow the traditional model are fundamentally different from those who are successful selling to big corporations today.

	Traditional Seller	Today's Seller
Priority	Getting the order	Making a difference
Focus	Opportunity fulfillment	Demand generation
Responsibility	Communicating value	Creating value
Differentiator	Product, service, or solution	Knowledge, expertise of seller

Priority

With *getting the order* as their top priority, traditional sellers create resistance in every customer interaction. People can intuitively feel when they're being sold. They can tell when someone is acting in a self-serving manner or is under intense pressure to deliver results. This self-created client resistance severely hampers the sales effectiveness of traditional sellers.

The priority of today's top sellers is *making a difference*. They see themselves as change agents who specialize in improving their customer's business. These sellers know that if they help their customers solve their problems and achieve their objectives, success automatically follows.

Focus

Traditional sellers are out there looking for "low-hanging fruit," customers with existing needs for their products and services who might be open to a change. They relish a meeting with decision makers to convince them why their offering is best. If that doesn't happen, they at least want a chance to submit a bid. Because they're always focused on *opportunity fulfillment,* they constantly fight price battles and struggle with differentiation.

Successful sellers today must focus on finding problem spots or missed opportunities inside their customer's operation that no other supplier is currently focused on. Once they identify these areas, they literally lead a sales campaign to help their prospect understand two things: (1) why change is an imperative and (2) why their solution is the answer. This *demand-generation* focus is proactive and provocative, as opposed to the traditional seller who simply responds to existing needs.

Responsibility

Traditional sellers see their role as being that of someone who *communicates the value* of their product or service. With their well-honed pitches, they can reel off their features, advantages, and benefits (FABs) one after the other. They love their brochures, samples, storyboards, or PowerPoint presentations. Blah, blah, blah. Or maybe a big yawn!

Sellers who are successful today know that customers can go online and find out all that stuff in seconds. They realize that they must *create value* with every customer interaction. They do this by helping clients see their business operations differently, by sharing useful information, by questioning the status quo, and by doing much more. They make customers think. They bring customers ideas and insights. Customers want to get together with these sellers because they always get something of value from the meetings.

Differentiator

Traditional sellers think that customers make decisions based on their *product, service, or solution* differentiators. They get frantic when they lack capabilities that competitors have or when their pricing is too high relative to what else is on the market.

Today's seller knows that their products, services, or solutions are simply tools—nothing more. They know that their customers could care less about buying new software or training their staff. They realize that customers invest in their offering because of the outcome they get. That's why their focus is on business improvement.

These top sellers are fully cognizant that *their knowledge and expertise* are the reasons that customers want to work with them. Traditional sellers don't have a clue that top sellers know so much more than they do about the market, operations, processes, competition, business goals and objectives, strategic imperatives, and more.

YOU'RE A REAL DIFFERENTIATOR

The reality is that in today's market, you personally make a huge difference. By bringing your knowledge, expertise, and ideas to the relationship, you separate yourself from all the product-pushing peddlers out there. Ultimately you become irresistible; customers want to do business with you.

I know a woman who sells soft goods to major retailers. Her product line is basically a commodity, and decision makers often use pricing as their primary criterion in selecting vendors. But not for this seller. She helps her customers increase their sales by:

- regularly shopping the competition and advising her retail customers about market trends;
- designing packaging alternatives and creative displays to encourage their customers to buy more at one time; and
- creating unique products for special occasions to drive additional revenue.

These tasks are *not* part of her job description. But because she willingly brings her knowledge of design, style, and business to the relationship, her customers reap huge benefits. Inventory turns faster and profits skyrocket.

As you can see, this goes far beyond just selling your products. It requires a very thoughtful, planned, and diligent approach to business. Top sellers know this and invest significantly more time deepening their knowledge base and expanding their expertise.

> Top sellers constantly think about how they can help customers improve their business.

Top sellers don't just service their accounts' needs, respond to customer questions, or prepare proposals that customers have requested. They're constantly focused on business improvement ideas. They proactively lead change initiatives with their customers. They challenge their customers' thinking and expand their range of possibilities. In short, top sellers are an incredible, indispensable asset to their client's business.

WHAT DECISION MAKERS WANT FROM YOU

Now that you understand the new model of what it takes to be successful in sales today, let's look at what that means specifically when you're attempting to get your foot in the door of big companies.

Focus Your Brain on Their Business

From the moment you target a big company, begin asking yourself these questions to help identify the difference you can make:

- How are they likely handling things relative to my offering?
- What are the potential problems they're encountering?
- What do I have in my tool kit that can have a positive impact on their business?
- What do I (people in my company) know about their industry, market, processes, workflow, and challenges that would be helpful to them? Why?

- How are their issues similar to other customers of mine?
- What might they have tried already to address these problems or achieve these goals?
- What strategic initiatives are already underway?

Please notice that none of these questions relates to selling. Everything is focused on business improvement. You're a change agent for them and you need to think like one. Engage your brain on your customer's challenges from the onset and you'll immediately position yourself as a valuable resource. Your thinking will be fundamentally different from that of anyone else asking for their valuable time.

Be Explicit in the Difference You Make

Those busy decision makers don't have one bit of time to intuit the impact you might have on their business. Corporate buyers could care less about the "bells and whistles" of your product, your unique methodology, or your impressive personal qualifications. They like the status quo. Until they clearly understand that change will have a really positive impact on their business, they won't budge.

So do the calculations for them. Quantify the difference you can make. Give them numbers, percents, time frames, and statistics. When you initially contact them, you need to shout out your value to them—loud and clear—so they can't miss it.

Personalize Every Contact

Corporate decision makers have absolutely no tolerance for sales spiels of any sort. If what you say in your conversations, voice mails, letters, e-mails, or any other form of communications sounds canned, you're a goner.

Every time you talk with them, you must make reference to something that indicates your knowledge of their specific business, industry, challenges, or operation. If you don't reference this knowledge, you won't have any credibility. Prospective customers take distinct notice of you when it's evident that you've done your homework.

Be a Provocateur

If you know your stuff, don't be afraid to show it. Often busy decision makers will brush you off as fast as they can because it's how they normally deal with sellers. They tell you that everything is fine, life is great, and that they're totally happy with what they're doing right now.

If you have researched their firm and have identified some differences you can make, don't let them get away with it. Quietly but confidently keep the focus on the business issues that you know they're dealing with. Use your depth of knowledge to discuss the ripple effect of these problems on their operation or processes.

In essence, be a consultant who has valuable ideas that are worth listening to. Make them think that perhaps you know something that could be of value. Again, please note, this is not a discussion about your product, service, or solution. It's a provocation around a business issue and the ramifications of their current operation.

Show Them How Others Do Things

Many people in big companies are isolated from the rest of the world. They're so busy working that they don't have time to keep up on what others are doing.

If you can be a good source of information to the corporate decision maker, you will be highly valued. They're especially interested in how similar companies have tackled the very same challenges they're facing. Any insights or ideas you can bring to the table are extremely valuable.

Talk with Them as Peers

Talking with customers on a peer level can feel pretty daunting if you're young or haven't worked with corporate decision makers before. Please realize that they're simply people trying to do the best they can. If you sound all goo-goo about talking with them, it hurts your credibility. Just focus on their business issues and the difference you can make and they'll be interested in meeting with you.

EMBRACE THE NEW SALES PARADIGM

When most sellers truly understand the new sales paradigm, they're excited about it. For the first time in a long while, they feel hope again. They're tired of fighting the rampant marketplace commoditization with the resulting price wars. But while most really do care about making a difference, what they don't understand is just how fundamental a shift they personally need to make.

The Bane of Your Sales Existence

Dropping solution-focused sales talk is much harder than most sellers think. I spend more time trying to rid sellers of their inveterate and compulsive need to talk about their great company, impressive offering, and wonderful service. Much as they hate pitching, it's so ingrained in their sales psyche that they don't even realize when they're doing it.

Your product or service is simply a tool. No one wants it in and of itself. You must get this firmly implanted in your head. Customers buy your product or service only because it helps them improve their business operation.

If you're trying to get into a big company, you can't focus on your offering. You may love it dearly. You may have developed it yourself. You may have spent weeks in training. You may think it's the greatest, but your prospective customers could care less. They're only thinking about their business, the issues and challenges they face, and how they can possibly achieve their objectives. This is where you must focus.

That means you must stop talking about your solution. That means you must stop trying to convince people that your company does a really great job. That means you have to eliminate all commentary about what great service you offer. Cleanse yourself of those bad habits right now. They're hurting your sales efforts.

The Experience of You

While your products and services may be nearly identical to others on the market, no one is the same as you. If you've worked hard to develop your expertise, you want customers to know that you possess a depth of knowledge and whole tool kit of products and services that can make a big difference for them.

Talking about it isn't enough. Think about when you were a teenager. Adults probably tried to share their hard-earned wisdom with you on numerous occasions. The more they talked "at" you, the less you listened. The louder they talked, the faster you turned them off. In order for anyone to penetrate your protective walls, they had to take a different approach.

The same thing holds true with corporate decision makers. They need to sense your confidence about making an impact without you piling it on. It's a quieter approach that's entirely focused on achieving the business results *they* want. It's driven by insightful, powerful questions that demonstrate your expertise. It's demonstrated by sharing the outcomes that your customers achieve.

When they're done talking with you, they must feel that their time has been well spent. They've thought about their business from a different perspective. They have ideas and insights that weren't there before you met. In short, they would willingly have paid $500 for that one-hour meeting with you because it was so valuable.

This formula expresses what sales is all about today:

Your Expertise + Your Offering = Business Improvement

As you read the rest of this book, you'll discover what you need to put in place at the front end of your sales efforts to get more business. You'll learn how to leverage your personal expertise and offering to target the right clients, set up initial meetings, and conduct those meetings like the professional you are.

Implementing these strategies is hard at first because you have to rewire your brain about what it takes to be successful in sales. Don't quit on yourself; keep going even though it's tough. The brutal reality is that if you don't change, it will be even more difficult for you. Just follow the very specific "how to" guidance in the upcoming chapters and you'll be well on your way to creating an extraordinarily successful future.

KEY POINTS

- In the new sales model, sellers focus on making a difference, improving their client's results, and solving problems.
- In order to build a relationship, you must create value with every single customer interaction.
- Corporate decision makers want you to bring them ideas, make them think, and expand their perspectives on what it takes to run their firm successfully.
- Continually developing your own knowledge base is critical for your long-term success; become a business improvement consultant.
- Make the "experience" of working with you fundamentally different from other sellers. Realize that *you* are the key differentiator.

Part Two

BUILD THE FOUNDATION

5

TARGETING: IT'S NOT A NUMBERS GAME

When you think about all the big companies out there, it's incredibly seductive to want to keep all your options open. After all, just about every corporation "could" use your products or services. And the more potential customers you have, the more sales you'll get. Right?

Not so. In fact, just the opposite is true. By narrowing your market focus, you increase sales and profits. Not by a little, but by a lot. For many people, this thinking is counterintuitive. It just doesn't feel right—especially if you're a new firm that's strapped for cash or a company that's struggling to redefine itself.

The last thing you want to do is walk away from any potential opportunity. But that's exactly what you must do! The question you must ask yourself is this: "Which big companies are most likely to buy your products or use your services?"

Selling to big companies is *not* a numbers game anymore. It's not about spending hours on the phone cold calling hundreds of people hoping to find someone who will meet with you. Selling today is about:

- targeting the types of businesses where you'll have a high likelihood of sales success;

- identifying a limited number of corporations that fit the parameters you've established; and
- investing all your sales time working on getting into those companies.

In other words, you pick the companies with whom you want to work and then make it happen.

SELECT YOUR FUTURE CUSTOMERS

Recently I talked to a consultant who shared with me that he was really struggling financially. Although he's been on his own for years, he's never managed to establish long-term relationships with corporate clients. Instead, he spends most of his time on the cash-poor small-business sector, trying to make it to the big time. When I asked about his target market, here's what he told me:

> "Big companies and small companies. It really doesn't matter what industry they're in. I've worked with real estate firms, insurance companies, professional services firms, and some of the big corporations in the city too.
>
> "I help them with team building, personal and career coaching, writing their marketing collateral, and sales training if they need it. Sometimes I even coach their executives. I like to tell people I'm a 'revenue coach.'"

Whew! Clearly this man wants to keep all his options open. He'll work with any company and do whatever they want him to—as long as he gets paid.

But how do corporate buyers react to him? Obviously, not well. In today's hypercompetitive market where they have an endless choice of possible suppliers, they want to work with experts who truly understand their business. They're so busy, they don't have time to bring people up to speed on their unique business issues and needs. They want to quickly assess if a seller's service or product is a good fit and move on. If a seller's message doesn't scream that it's a perfect fit for them, the seller is immediately eliminated from consideration.

That's why defining *your* target market is so important. In fact, when you're clear about it, you can craft a powerful value proposition that entices your ideal customer so much that they'll want to learn more about your offering—soon!

Well-defined target markets increase the effectiveness of your marketing and sales efforts too because everything you do is focused on that targeted customer. Prospective buyers "feel" like you understand their business, industry, challenges, and concerns in greater depth. They perceive you and your company as having greater expertise and superior products.

When you know your target market well, you know the trade shows they attend, the magazines and trade journals they read, the Web sites they visit, and more. You invest less money on your sales and marketing with significantly improved results. Because prospective customers can find you more easily, referrals go up. Finally, you differentiate your business from competitors, thus increasing your profitability.

As Geoffrey Moore vividly points out in *Crossing the Chasm,* companies that try to be "all things to all people" have significantly higher costs, never really establish a strong customer base from which to grow, and often disappear before achieving profitable growth. If you're like most people, though, it's really hard to walk away from any potential business. Yet closing the door on some opportunities truly opens far more doors for you in others.

DEFINE THE DEMOGRAPHICS

The first key to success in selling to big companies is to clearly define your ideal customer. Often when I ask people to tell me about this perfect client, I hear comments such as:

- "They need what we offer."
- "They're ready to buy."
- "They really want to work with us."
- "They don't panic when we say how much it costs."
- "They appreciate the kind of work we do."
- "They pay their bills quickly."

Certainly we'd all like those kinds of customers. But a target market is much more than this. It's a group of prospective customers who, because they share common characteristics, are *especially receptive* to your products or services.

What are these "common characteristics?" Start out by defining the *demographics* or the basic facts about the types of companies you work with best. There are many ways you can determine the demographics of your ideal customer profile. For example, you might want to ask yourself these questions:

- What industry are they in? Are they manufacturing firms or services businesses? Are they in telecom, medical devices, health care, or software?
- How big are they? What are their revenues? How many employees do they have? Are they a regional firm or global?
- What are their distribution channels? Do they use direct sales? Distribution organizations? Online sales or catalogs?
- What type of technology base do they utilize? What are their existing computer systems? Manufacturing processes?
- Who are their customers? Do they sell in the business-to-business marketplace, business-to-consumer, or business-to-channel?
- What is their development stage? Are they in the growth mode? Are they a mature organization? Or is their business declining?

When I started my company years ago, I was pretty naïve about target markets. I willingly worked with anyone who needed sales training. In my first year, I trained people who sold insurance to consumers, industrial pumps to manufacturers, cereal products to food service establishments, heart monitors to physicians, and attorneys trying to get corporate business.

Each contract was a one-off project requiring hours of time spent studying their products, services, markets, customer needs, and the selling strategies of their top performers. I felt like I was getting paid peanuts for the amount of time I invested with each customer.

My business took off when I finally came to my senses and decided to leverage my expertise. All my sales experience and success was with technology firms in the business-to-business (B2B) sector. I talked their language, understood their issues, and established immediate credibility with decision makers in B2B companies.

The same thing happened to InTouch, Inc., one of the thousands of telemarketing firms out there today. Ever since CEO Brian Carroll and his management team got a clear focus on their target market, business has gone steadily uphill. With whom do they work? They target companies with a long-term, complex sales cycle. They also have very specific parameters related to annual revenue and sales force size as well.

Without a well-defined target market, it's much harder to be successful selling to large accounts. I'll never forget the day one of my customers, a company that specialized in products for the scientific community, gleefully announced changes enabling their sales force to call on financial services firms, hospitals, and government institutions. I was stunned with this irresponsible decision. Six months later, everyone's initial euphoria had totally evaporated as sales fell to an all-time low.

Big companies don't have time to educate sellers regarding their marketplace. They want to work with people who are knowledgeable in their industry. A friend of mine used to work for a custom-designed training company with absolutely no focus. When he decided to target pharmaceutical firms, his business blossomed. He learned the lingo, knew when they needed his services, and could intelligently discuss what was happening in the industry.

If your firm doesn't have a target market, create your own by focusing on specific types of customers. If you don't have a specialization, you can create that too. You have to start somewhere!

SCOPE OUT THE PSYCHOGRAPHICS

It's imperative to determine the *psychographics* of your target market as well as the demographics. These intangible factors help you assess if a prospective customer is the right "fit" for your business. These characteristics are every bit as important as the factual data because they're what make the relationship work. Questions you can ask to determine the psychographics of your target market include:

- What are the vision and values of the organization? How about the character and ethos of the firm? How committed are they to their people, customers, or the environment?
- What is their reputation in the industry? Are they innovators or low cost providers? Are they early adopters of technology or laggards?
- What are their management priorities? What's most important to them—increasing sales, cutting costs, or improving operational efficiency? What are their critical success factors?
- How would you evaluate their perceptions of your industry, product, or service offering? Positive, negative, neutral?
- How would you define their management style? Are they top-down driven? Do they encourage individual and team contributions?

It's harder to determine these intangible elements, especially if you're on the outside looking in. However, you can find clues to the psychographics of big corporations by reading what they say about their own firm on their Web sites, in marketing collateral, and in their annual report. You can learn more by checking out what industry analysts say about the company in online forums or in trade publications. Past and current employees are also great sources of information.

To determine the psychographics that work best for your firm, take a good look at your existing customers. Some have been difficult to work with from the beginning. Others keep using more and more of your products and services, and you love working with them. Figure out what's different between these two categories. Then pursue working with the kinds of clients where you know you have a better chance of winning the business.

Personally, I won't work with certain types of firms because I don't like their ethics or I don't like what they sell. Military contractors and tobacco companies aren't in my target market. Nor are slow-moving companies who sell commodities. I overwhelm them with ideas; they drive me crazy with their plodding nature. On the other hand, I truly enjoy working with companies focused on growth, who believe their salespeople are their prime differentiators in the marketplace and who like to try new things.

That intangible factor of "fit" is all about alignment. It makes a huge difference.

EVALUATE THE ENABLING CONDITIONS

Your best target markets are those where the *enabling conditions* are ripe for what you're selling. Your offering helps them achieve their critical business objectives or solves a problem they're currently facing.

After defining the right demographics and psychographics of my target market, I realized that my best customers all had one thing in common: new product launches were critical to their success. They loved their technology way too much, and their sellers couldn't wait to talk with prospective customers about all its wonderful capabilities. This created massive problems in their sales efforts. Marketing rarely gave the sales force what they needed to be effective in selling. Consequently, it invariably took much too long for new product sales to ramp up in the marketplace. That meant delayed time-to-revenue, a fairly critical business issue.

The minute I focused on this much-narrowed market segment, my business skyrocketed. My target market immediately understood what I could do for them and why it was important. I was busy for ten years—nonstop! That's the power of having a clearly defined target market.

Discover Goals, Objectives, and Strategic Imperatives

If you analyze your best customers, you may find out that one thing they have in common is that they're pursuing a specific direction that just happens to create opportunities for your offering. Perhaps they're focused on:

- entering new markets,
- growing sales, revenue, or market share,
- improving operational efficiency,
- reducing cost of goods sold,
- shrinking their time to market,
- outsourcing nonessential functions,
- establishing strategic partnerships and alliances,
- streamlining the supply chain, or
- redefining their go-to-market strategies.

Identify Challenges, Issues, or Problems

Another way to determine the best enabling conditions for your offering is to identify the common challenges, issues, or problems that your product or service solves. What were your best clients struggling with before they worked with your firm? What problems were they having? Perhaps they were facing issues such as:

- Declining profitability, poor sales, and stagnant growth
- Delayed time-to-market of new products
- Inefficient processes and poor productivity
- Inability to make decisions
- Increased competition and pricing pressures
- Difficulty in implementing key initiatives
- Poor internal and external communications
- Declining market share
- Finding good employees
- Implementing new governmental regulations
- Changes in customer requirements
- Industry trends threatening their market position
- Integrating multiple distribution channels

Any commonality you identify helps you get more focused on your ideal client profile.

NAME THAT NICHE

Defining your target market is one of the most important things you can do to increase your sales to big companies. And it's one of the very first things you should do! After all, if you don't know what kinds of customers you work with best, you might not recognize an opportunity even when it's staring you in the face.

If this strategy is new to you, don't worry about crafting a perfect definition of your target market. But you do need to hone your target market down to something that you can get your hands around. Use Tool 1: Target Market Definition in Appendix A to record the demographics, psychographics, and enabling conditions of those clients that are ideal for your business. If this is difficult for you to do right now, Appendix A also contains these tools that may help you more clearly define your best target market:

- Tool 2: Past Customer Analysis
- Tool 3: Offering Assessment
- Tool 4: Personal Credibility Appraisal

As you learn more about your marketplace, make the course corrections you find necessary. Realize that your niche may evolve over the years—especially if you run your own business. Your personal interests may change over time. Market conditions may change, causing you to refocus your efforts. Even your clients can cause you to change—the "one-off" project you do for them expands your knowledge base, creating new opportunities for you.

Once you've defined your target market, then identify the names of actual companies that align closely with the parameters you've established. If you're like many people, you want to list all the large corporations located close by. It doesn't work that way. You have to pick the right companies, near or far, to pursue.

I live in a metropolitan area with lots of big companies. There's a temptation to be a nondiscriminating seller. Target, 3M, General Mills, Carlson Companies, and Cargill are just of few of the biggies in my backyard. Yet I would be wasting immeasurable time and effort if I pursued business with all of them. Why? To the best of my knowledge, only two of these big companies fit my ideal client profile.

Don't be promiscuous in your prospecting. Be selective. Use the target market criteria you've established to identify the Top Ten big companies you'd like to work with in the next year.

What? Only ten companies? Yes, you heard me correctly. There's no way you can do justice to more than ten big companies. You have so much to learn about them first. There's research to do, account entry strategies to plan, and people to meet. You're just getting started.

Please don't get me wrong. You can contact more than ten companies, but your brain can only really focus on a select number of A-priority firms—big companies where you can establish a beachhead that will lead to lots of future business.

The most important thing to remember about target marketing is this: "Just do it!" The sooner the better. Stop working harder than you have to. Stop spending way too much time and money trying to reach a broad base of customers who "could" use your product or services, but who don't have the compelling needs that others do. Stop the endless prospecting and begging for people's attention.

Claim your target market now. Own it. Be the specialist, keep developing your expertise, and look for ways to grow your business within your segment. And just as important to your sale success with big companies—*walk away* from all opportunities that aren't in your target market.

KEY POINTS

- Narrowing your market focus and closing the door on some opportunities results in increased sales and profitability.
- Buyers in today's hypercompetitive markets have an endless choice of suppliers. They prefer to work with experts who understand their business.
- Clearly define the demographics and psychographics of your ideal target market. Be as specific as possible so you can reduce the number of companies you'll pursue.
- Analyze your existing customers to define the enabling conditions that make a company ripe for what you're selling.
- Once you've determined the exact parameters of your "best fit" clients, identify ten companies, maximum, that align most closely with these characteristics.

6

IS YOUR VALUE PROPOSITION STRONG ENOUGH?

If you're struggling to get into big companies, you probably have a weak value proposition. Pure and simple. Your vague or nebulous statements about the benefits that customers get from using your product or service are likely the root cause of your account entry problems.

After you define your target market, the next thing to do is to clarify your value proposition. Without a strong value proposition that's highly attractive to your targeted buyers, it's hard to get in to meet with corporate decision makers. But what exactly is a value proposition? And how is it different from other commonly used terms?

A value proposition answers these questions for prospective customers: "How can you help my business? What difference do you make?"

A *value proposition* is a clear statement of the tangible results a customer gets from using your products or services. It is focused on outcomes and stresses the business value of your offering.

A strong value proposition is just what you need to get your foot in the door of big companies and create opportunities to sell your products or services. A value proposition is financially oriented and speaks to the critical issues your target market is facing. A strong value proposition is specific, often citing numbers or percentages. It may include a quick synopsis of your work with similar customers as a proof source and demonstration of your capability.

WHY ELEVATOR SPEECHES AND UNIQUE SELLING PROPOSITIONS ARE BOTH WORTHLESS

While a value proposition is often confused with an elevator speech or a unique selling proposition, its purpose and sales impact are fundamentally different when selling to big companies.

An *elevator speech* answers the question: "What do you do?" It's a short, one-sentence or two-sentence statement that defines who you work with (your target market) and the general area in which you help them. The following elevator speeches show you how some sellers describe what they do:

> "My company works with small businesses that are struggling to sell their products or services into large corporate accounts."

> "We help technology companies effectively use their customer information to drive repeat sales."

> "I help small-sized to medium-sized manufacturing companies who have difficulties with unpredictable revenue streams."

Typically, elevator speeches are about ten seconds long. They're used primarily at networking events to attract potential clients and stimulate discussion. Because decision makers from big companies rarely attend these events, elevator speeches have minimal impact on your ability to get in. An elevator speech is the foundation of a value proposition without the specificity that is needed to sell into the corporate market.

A *unique selling proposition (USP)* answers the question: "How is your company different from the other vendors?" Its primary purpose is to create competitive differentiation. Here are several examples of USPs:

"We specialize in working with financial institutions." (specialty)

"We guarantee service in less than four hours or your money back." (guarantee)

"We use a unique tool called SureFire! to analyze your critical needs." (methodology)

Helping customers understand your USP is imperative once they've decided to make a purchase decision. But USPs have absolutely no impact on customers who don't want to change. That's why USPs don't work when used to get into big companies.

Both the elevator speech and the USP are cousins of the value proposition, but both lack its punch for capturing the attention of corporate decision makers. In short, they're worthless.

WEAK VALUE PROPOSITIONS ARE EPIDEMIC

I'm continually amazed at how most sellers respond when I ask how their product or service helps big companies. Based on their answers, you'd think I'd asked an entirely different question. They can wax poetic about what they sell or what they do for a living. But they can't tell me the difference their offering makes to corporate buyers. While their products or services may actually deliver high value, their inability to articulate that value prevents them from getting in.

People who sell products are notorious for expounding on their USPs, those capabilities that differentiate them from competitors, as seen in these examples:

"We offer the most robust technologically advanced system in the market today with the widest range of capabilities available."

"Our system was rated best in class at the recent Big Deal Conference sponsored by the Elitist Consulting Group."

"We're the low-cost provider of this kind of product."

"We offer one-stop shopping. Our company has a full range of products to meet your every need in this area."

Boring! When most corporate decision makers hear these types of comments, they yawn and then say, "So what? Why should I waste my valuable time talking to you?"

These weak value propositions contain absolutely no measurable, quantifiable business results. Plus, any time people hear words such as *best, leading,* and *superior,* they immediately dismiss them as self-promoting aggrandizement. These trite, self-serving words actually detract from your message.

Most service firms aren't any better. They just have a different way of mucking up their value propositions. They love to tell you all the things they can do. You'd likely hear them describe their value proposition as:

"We're an OD consultancy specializing in visioning, team building, strategy development, and process engineering."

"We design brochures, Web sites, and packaging materials and can handle all your branding and identity needs."

"We're a sales training firm, and we offer a full range of courses covering all aspects of the sales process."

What's wrong with these value propositions? They're simply informative. They don't tie in what they do with any business results. These sellers just dump out an overview of their firm, hoping the client will make that intuitive leap to why their services are needed at this particular moment in time. As you know by now, this never happens.

Worse yet are the "ramblers" who want to throw out everything they do, hoping that the more they say, something will stick. Here's how their value proposition might sound:

"We do process reengineering with the various departments, divisions, business units, and subsidiaries from organizations as well as the numerous contractors that provide
products and services that go into the development of your own
branded and unbranded products. We initially start by doing a
comprehensive assessment of the multiple groups involved in
the process, covering questions such as . . ."

While these ramblers certainly know their stuff, they're not talking
in a language that a customer wants to hear. Their long-winded wordi-
ness is of no interest to busy corporate buyers. Period.

DESCRIBE TANGIBLE, MEASURABLE BUSINESS OUTCOMES

To break through the marketing clutter, your value proposition
must be stated in business terms. Remember, corporate decision makers
don't care about your product's speed, specifications, or efficiency.
They don't care about the wonderful methodology you use.

> Your offering is simply a tool. Decision makers care only about the
> results your offering delivers for them.

What Decision Makers Love to Hear

Corporate buyers are particularly attracted to phrases that are
linked to their business goals and objectives. Start speaking in these
terms and you'll definitely attract their attention:

- Increased revenues or profitability
- Faster time to market
- Decreased costs
- Improved operational efficiency
- Integrating operations globally

- Revitalizing the organization
- Enhancing customer loyalty
- Integrating e-commerce into marketing and sales
- Increased market share
- Decreased employee turnover
- Improved customer retention levels
- Increased competitive differentiation
- Faster response time
- Decreased operational expenses
- Increased sales per customer
- Improved asset utilization
- Faster collections
- Reduced cost of goods sold
- Minimized risk
- Additional revenue streams
- Increased market share
- Improved time-to-profitability
- Increased billable hours
- Reduced cycle time
- Increased inventory turns
- Faster sales cycles
- Reduced direct labor costs

Can your business do any of these things? How about something similar? Perhaps you never really thought about your products or services from this perspective. But because this is what corporate decision makers listen for, make sure to integrate these business-oriented terms into your value proposition.

Specificity Sells

The more specific your value proposition, the more attractive it is to decision makers. The very best value propositions deliver tangible, measurable results that are highly desirable to prospective buyers.

Yet many companies fail to extend their "benefits" into actual numbers. If it's possible for you to quantify the value your offering delivers, I highly recommend it. Stories are another way of providing specificity, enabling you to get your message across without making unsubstantiated, across-the-board claims.

When my "Winning More Sales" manual was published, one of the first people to purchase it wrote me a note saying that my advice helped him land a $26,000 sale the very next day. With his permission, I use that quote to promote my manual because it makes the manual's price seem miniscule when it is compared to the value received!

I recently read an article about a company whose software calculates exactly how much retailers should charge to "squeeze the maximum profit from every product and at any time." The article explained that during an eight-week test with one retailer, the retailer's revenues jumped 10 percent, unit volume increased 6 percent, and net profit grew 2 percent due to the software's price-optimization capabilities. Payback was expected within 12 months.

What retailer wouldn't want to learn more about what this software company does! As I was reading the article, I could practically see the retailer's senior management team salivating over the information in it. That's what a great value proposition does. Prospective customers should be able to visualize exactly what value you bring to their organization.

Notice the specificity of the software company's value proposition, its use of business-oriented language, and its focus on key business metrics. Powerful, isn't it? Their salespeople will certainly open a lot more doors with it than if they told prospects, "We sell price optimization software."

This software firm actually has multiple value propositions, as do most products and services. So when you're looking for your value proposition, don't just stop with one. Identify all the differences that you make so you have a multitude to choose from. Then, based on the account you're pursuing and what you learn about their business, you can craft your value proposition for maximum impact.

Measure the Tangible Value

When you're defining your value proposition, first examine where the impact of your offering can most easily be quantified. Tangible value is typically expressed in numbers, percentages, and time frames. Examples might be:

- Reduce cycle time from three days to one
- Cut labor costs by 25 percent
- Save $100,000 in energy costs
- Increase market share 5 percent
- Improving productivity 17 percent

Typically these tangible gains also have related indirect value gains that aren't quite as obvious, but they can help strengthen an already strong value proposition. For example, improving productivity means fewer workers. With a smaller workforce, the company saves a significant amount on benefit costs. Less money is spent in recruiting and hiring. These savings can also be quantified as part of your value proposition.

A well-designed Web site may cut the need for customer service staff. A more efficient just-in-time (JIT) ordering process decreases the amount of warehouse space and its associated costs. A digital asset management system's ability to repurpose data reduces advertising expenditures. Always try to quantify the indirect values as well as the direct ones.

Spell Out Intangible Value

Sometimes the value of your offering is not quite so easy to measure. Perhaps you help companies lower risk, increase teamwork, enhance marketplace image, or improve morale. Maybe your products are eco-friendly or made by disabled workers. Intangible value doesn't sell well in today's hypercompetitive marketplace. Most decision makers consider it a nice added benefit, but they won't spend money for a solution that provides only intangible value.

To increase your sales success, take these intangibles and make them tangible. For example, if morale is improved, fewer sick days are taken and employee turnover is reduced. If what you sell has much intangible value, it's imperative to find ways to quantify it.

Outline Opportunity Costs

An *opportunity cost* is something your customers can't do now because their current methods of operation preclude it. You can integrate opportunity costs into your value propositions. For example, outline what they could be doing with the $500,000 savings they'd get from using your product. Or itemize the business strategy and associated profits they can't aggressively pursue because of the internal conflicts that delay decisions.

As its title suggests, Tool 5: Clarify Your Value Proposition in the Account Entry Tool Kit in Appendix A provides a worksheet to help you better define and strengthen your value proposition.

THE IRRESISTIBLE ATTRACTION OF POWERFUL VALUE PROPOSITIONS

Not long ago, I had lunch with the president of a half-billion-dollar division of a major corporation. She told me that if a seller approached her and said he could reduce waste by just 1 percent, she would meet with him immediately. Why? Because she knew exactly how much her company spent on waste, and it was a lot of money. Every penny she saved would go right to the bottom line.

Powerful value propositions open doors—quickly! Making the effort to clarify your value propositions is well worth the time invested in the process. If you can't get specific numbers, at least talk business terminology.

Here are several well-crafted value propositions that have proven extremely effective in opening the doors of large corporate accounts.

> "We help large companies reduce the cost of their employee benefits programs without impacting benefit levels. With the spiraling costs of health care today, this is a critical issue. One of our recent clients saved over $800,000 in just six months without cutting any services to their employees or making them pay more."
>
> – Benefits Firm

> "After working with our firm, one well-known retailer saw a 54 percent increase in sales conversions and a 25 percent increase in average order size from their online sales. Our clients typically see 40 percent to 150 percent improvements in key operating metrics such as profit margins, rates, and cost savings."
>
> – Web Design Company

> "We help technology companies significantly shorten time-to-profitability and meet projected sales goals for their new product launches."
> — Sales Consultancy

I recently pulled a 5" × 5" multipage insert out of a magazine that featured four real-life stories from Google advertisers who figured out "how to reach their audience at the right moment with the best idea—even with a small ad budget." On the left side of each spread was the entrepreneur in his and her business setting. On the right was an overview of the results they achieved.

One woman turned her hobby into a seven-figure company by using keyword advertising. Sales rose 20 percent monthly, while her ad costs dropped from 20 percent to 5 percent of revenue.

Another man switched from running newspaper advertising to using Google's AdWords. His Web site traffic quadrupled in just six months, his leads increased fivefold, and he gets at least ten contacts a day from active buyers.

Impressive business results coupled with real-life stories are irresistible to corporate buyers. That's what value propositions are all about. They attract. They magnetize. They open doors. They get you into big companies.

HOW TO USE YOUR VALUE PROPOSITION

Corporate decision makers will nearly always meet with sellers who speak their language, focus on helping them achieve their objectives, and talk about tangible, measurable business results. You'll immediately notice a change in how you're treated when you find the right words to describe your offering. Customizing your value proposition to a prospect's specific business needs and goals takes it to an even higher level of attraction.

Strong value propositions are the foundation of all your sales and marketing efforts. Once you clearly define your value proposition, you can use it to:

- craft a telephone script that highlights the key business results your product, service, or solution delivers;

- write a business letter to decision makers who work at targeted accounts;
- establish a basis for your marketing campaign and in all your marketing collateral;
- build the foundation for customer-centric PowerPoint presentations; and
- develop the core message delivered in your totally customized customer proposals.

But based on what I've seen in working with sellers, the biggest benefit you get from understanding your value proposition is . . . (drum roll) . . . a strengthened belief in your own offering.

When you truly understand the business value you bring to customers, you work harder to get into accounts. You're less discouraged by rejection. You don't question if there's a market for what you sell. Ultimately when you know your product or service makes a valuable difference, you sell a lot more!

KEY POINTS

- Weak value propositions are the root cause of most sellers' inability to get into large corporations.
- Strong value propositions focused on the business value that companies get from using your product or service are of high interest to corporate decision makers.
- Specificity sells. Include numbers, percents, dollars, and time frames to make your value proposition stronger and more credible.
- A value proposition can include tangible value, intangible value, and opportunity costs. Different prospects may be interested in different aspects of the value your offering provides.
- Remember, your product or service is simply a tool. Buyers want it because of the results they get from using it.

7

STRENGTHEN YOUR VALUE PROPOSITION

So how does your own value proposition look? If it's not strong enough yet, don't despair. As I said earlier, most people and companies have a much more powerful one than they use. They just get caught up describing "what" they make or "how" they do things.

Your challenge is to create a value proposition so enticing that when corporate decision makers hear it, they say, "I need to learn more." While this may seem glaringly obvious, in real life it can be much more difficult to implement.

Recently I talked with a woman who said she did training for sales organizations. As a nosy but friendly competitor, I asked about her programs. She told me they were based on the appreciative inquiry model that builds upon what salespeople already do right. When I asked about the outcome of her methodology, she replied, "It energizes the sales force."

After 25 years in this field, I've never met a sales executive who wanted their salespeople to have more "energy." They want results—pure and simple. More orders. Fewer losses to the competition. Bigger or more profitable contracts. Better customer retention. If you're selling to sales management, you need to use these terms.

FIND THE POWER OF YOUR
VALUE PROPOSITION

Clarifying value propositions isn't just hard for individuals. Sometimes entire companies seem to create value propositions in a vacuum. They blindly go to market without testing how customers perceive their marketing messages.

Several years ago I worked with a large corporation that introduced a new system into the printing market. They were ecstatic about its extraordinary color matching capabilities that were far superior to anything else out there. The "dots" on the page were of such high quality, they just knew that printers would flock to do business with their firm.

However, sales stalled out after the early adopters made the conversion. I was asked to help on a relaunch. In the process, I interviewed a number of their customers. One printer had metrics on every aspect of its business. I learned that by using the new "color" product, this printer:

- cut the staff in their prepress area by 33 percent and still handled the same workload;
- redeployed these valuable workers to other areas of the firm (where they were desperately needed) and cut overtime costs;
- reduced project turnaround time by two to three days, creating a significant competitive advantage and enabling them to pick up some key clients; and
- balanced out their workflow, allowing them to delay the purchase of an expensive new press.

This was my client's true value proposition. It was strong. Really strong. Their offering created positive business results in many areas, but they didn't see it because they were fixated on "great color," a proposition that wasn't selling. Their customers were too busy to translate the implications of this superior color technology into quantifiable business results, something that needed to be done in order to justify their investment. Within one year of learning their true value proposition, my client reached 50 percent market share.

Guidelines for Strong Value Propositions

- Talk outcomes, not products or processes
- Tie results to critical business issues
- Use business terminology
- Include metrics or statistics
- Refer to actual client successes

Get the Inside Scoop

Your existing customers are a veritable fountain of information regarding the business value of your product or service. They're unequivocally the best resource you can use to clarify your value proposition.

If you're new to sales or to your company, talking with existing customers needs to be a priority. Set up meetings with them as soon as you can. If you've been around for a while, an in-depth customer interview provides you with a fresh perspective that can take your sales to a new level. If you're selling your own services, by interviewing your own clients you gain valuable insights into what they deem important.

To get these appointments, ask your customers for their assistance. Tell them you want to learn about the value of your offering to their organization and how it helps them run their business better. Assure them that you're looking to understand their business in greater depth so you can be of better service to them in the future. These discussions enhance your relationship with customers at the same time they give you a chance to learn an incredible amount of insider information.

Going into these interviews, your mindset must be that you're simply there to ask questions and learn. Don't sell during the interview under any circumstances. Even if an opportunity drops in your lap, put it aside till you've asked all your questions. By all means, take copious notes! Be curious. Explore your customer's answers in depth to learn the extent of the value you provide. Be inquisitive and interested. Search for the information you need in order to get a firm handle on your value proposition.

Following are questions you can ask to determine your true value proposition. Be aware that your customers may not have thought much, if at all, about the value you provide. Therefore, the responses you hear may initially seem like little help in clarifying your value proposition.

Remain conversational and curious. Gently poke and prod your customer to explore different areas. People need and deserve time to think things through. Agitating them by demanding that they talk about tangible business results right away won't help you at all.

Have you ever seen any old Columbo movies or TV reruns? If so, remember how Columbo, a wily detective who knew a whole lot more than he let on, slowly and softly kept asking questions until he found what he was looking for. Emulating Columbo's modus operandi will have a high payback for you.

Customer Interview Questions

Consider the questions below as a guideline for your customer meeting. To get better data, customize your questions to your product or service offering. Both tangible values and intangible values need to be considered as you work on strengthening your value proposition. If your customer shares a tough-to-measure result, such as improved communications, brainstorm on how to make the business value tangible.

- Before you started using our offering, how did you handle things?
  - Why did you decide to change to or to use our service?
  - What problems were you hoping it would solve?
  - What objectives were you expecting it to help you achieve?
- On a scale of 1 to 10, how would you rate our offering in terms of helping you reach your desired result? Why did you select this rating?
- Did you realize any positive results that surprised you?
- What were the three most important benefits you received as a result of our product/work together?
- What value did our offering provide to your company? How would you quantify the value of these improvements?
- How did it impact . . . ? What were its ramifications on . . . ? What was the effect on . . . ?
- What improvements did you realize? How did that help your bottom line or with your growth objectives?

- What did our solution enable you to do that you couldn't before?
- What is doing that worth to your organization?
- What other areas in your company benefited because of our work together?
- Can you help me quantify the payoff your firm realized from using our offering?

Ask these same questions to more than one person in your customer's organization. Talk to people in different areas and in different positions in the company. They each have a unique and highly valuable perspective. Sometimes you'll hear something totally new from one person that will lead you to a much stronger value proposition.

If your customers say negative things about you, your offering, or your company, listen and ask questions. While this is not what you wanted to get from these meetings, it is critical data. Don't get defensive, make excuses, pass the blame, or tell your customers that they're wrong. If you do, they'll shut down fast and you'll lose all credibility. At times like this, what's most important is maintaining the business relationship. While you can't always guarantee positive outcomes, customers still appreciate the opportunity to give feedback and have their frustrations heard.

CAPITALIZE ON YOUR COLLECTIVE WISDOM

Another way to clarify your value proposition is by brainstorming with your colleagues. The collective wisdom and experience of your peers provides a broad overview on the value of your offering from a customer's perspective. Review your marketing materials. Reflect on what you know about your customers. Think about what you say that interests and excites them.

As a group, here are some questions you can discuss:

- What problems does our product, service, or solution solve?
- How do these problems impact other parts of the company?
- How does our product, service, or solution affect our customer's bottom line or expenses?

- What positive impact has our offering had on bringing additional revenue and business to our clients?
- Does our offering enable our customers to achieve a competitive advantage? If so, how?
- Does our offering have a positive impact on our customer's customers? If so, what?

If your group is struggling to identify tangible results, challenge yourself to take the discussion to the next level. Keep asking each other, "So what?"

- So what if it's an efficient system?
- So what if they have improved communication?
- So what if we cut turnaround time by two days?

Asking these questions over and over again gets you much closer to the real value you bring to customers. Look for the impact your offering has on their organization. Explore the financial effect your products, systems, or services have on their business.

Quantify, quantify, quantify. Where are the dollar savings? How can you measure the increased productivity? How much have you increased sales? The more you can make your value proposition tangible, the easier it will be to get your foot in the door of big companies.

Determining your value proposition with only an internal analysis can be dangerous, though. Outside validation by your customers is far more important. It doesn't matter what your marketing department thinks is valuable. When it comes down to spending money, it's only the perception of your customers that counts.

If you're an independent professional, get a group of colleagues together and brainstorm each other's business cases. You need their perspectives to clarify your primary value proposition. You're much too close to it to discover it without help.

WHAT IF YOU DON'T HAVE METRICS?

Many consultants and professional services providers find it difficult to quantify the measurable results customers realize from using their offerings. Because of this, they think they can't come up with a strong value proposition.

I understand their frustrations. With 15 years of consulting under my belt, none of my product launch clients measured the effectiveness of my work. There were many reasons for this: not enough time to compare before-and-after results, lack of benchmarking, and the multiple factors that can impact a new product's market success. So like many of you, I lacked good hard data.

However, this didn't stop me from talking about what I did in business terms. Rather than giving exact figures (which was impossible), I emphasized the:

- lag time between product launch and achieving projected sales results;
- critical need to shorten time-to-revenue;
- high costs of sales representative downtime spent on preparing presentations and proposals;
- lost windows of opportunity, enabling competitive inroads; and
- inconsistent messages being delivered to channel partners and customers.

These value propositions were extremely attractive to senior marketing and sales leaders. As a result, I had a highly profitable new product launch consulting practice for years.

Speak the Language of Business

Talking as a businessperson talks is where you have to start. For example, if your company designs Web sites, put on your thinking cap to figure out what a corporate decision maker might be interested in. Honestly, they don't care about your awards or how long you've been in business.

To catch their attention, you might want to focus your discussions with them on:

- driving more traffic to the Web site;
- decreasing the number of customers abandoning full shopping carts;

- increasing the transaction value per customer;
- improving search engine rankings; and
- freeing up corporate resources through improved online capabilities.

Whatever profession you're in, it's critical to talk about your work in business terminology. As a result of working with you, what are the outcomes? What business results are attained? They're there! You just need to find them.

Extend Existing Business Statistics

Just because you don't have statistics doesn't mean you can't get them. Perhaps your customers already have metrics you could benchmark against.

Rita Webster, president of WiseLeader, coaches executives who want to accomplish more through the people they lead. One of her manufacturing clients had great statistics on their output and rework. Consequently, they were able to compare how things were before her consulting and after. As a result of working with her, the client realized:

- 31 percent increases in productivity;
- 12 percent decreases in scrap per unit; and
- 37 percent drops in materials and labor per unit.

When she talks to prospective customers, Rita can reference these statistics as well as the fact that she helps her clients:

- eliminate management time spent on handling employee conflict;
- streamline processes to increase operational efficiency; and
- minimize destructive turf issues that cost companies millions each year as management scrambles for power.

While Rita does a lot of one-on-one coaching and teambuilding—sometimes considered warm and fuzzy stuff—she knows her work has a profound impact on their business because she has the statistics to back it up.

Engage New Customers in Measurement

Think about how you might demonstrate your value with your upcoming sales opportunities. Skip Jankoski, President of FreshSuccess, Inc., does this regularly. His specialty marketing business development firm specializes in helping salespeople establish new clients.

Skip never talks about the creativity of their "engagement system." Instead, he focuses on the client's business objectives for lead generation. Early in the sales process he talks to decision makers about what to measure and how they'll do it. Their metrics can be as simple as tracking:

- who received the package,
- if the seller got an appointment,
- if a new sale was made,
- the initial value of the sale, and
- the projected client value over time.

His customers immediately know if their investment was worthwhile. Plus the business metrics he gets can easily be leveraged as success stories for future sales efforts or as strong case studies that support his value proposition.

If you currently lack statistics, think about how you might engage your customers in creating measurement systems that are helpful to them and you. Your efforts in this area can have huge paybacks for you.

Use Industry Statistics

The truth is that sometimes it's difficult or nearly impossible to measure the value of what you do. If this happens to be your situation, I strongly recommend using industry statistics. You can also use statistics to support your value proposition, providing the "outside expert" perspective that gives you even more clout.

Here are several examples of how industry statistics might be incorporated into your value proposition:

- To get in to see prospective clients, I frequently mention a study that says, "75 percent of executives who work for big companies involved in a complex sale blame poor value propositions as a major cause of their new products failing to achieve sales projections."

- One of my friends is a consultant who does a lot of work for big companies in the area of teamwork. The statistic she uses is that "50 percent of a manager's time is spent resolving people problems related to trust issues and poor communications."

If you think about your business, I suspect you can come up with some industry statistics also. Again, they can be great proof sources of the need for your product or service in the market.

TEST YOUR VALUE PROPOSITION

Before you begin contacting corporate decision makers, it's imperative to clarify your value proposition. Otherwise, no matter how hard you try, you'll be ineffective in your attempts to get in.

Realize too that you may not be a good judge of your own value proposition. The only person who can truly make that determination is a decision maker in your targeted market. If you have a strong relationship with some clients, run your value proposition by them. Find out:

- Does it interest them? If so, why? If not, why not?
- What did they find most compelling? Why?
- What did they think was boring, weak or unimportant?

If you can't interview a customer, try the next best thing—a simulated client. Pick a colleague or a person as close to your prospective buyer as possible. Lay the groundwork by giving them an overview of your target market and some information on your decision maker's objectives and concerns. Give them a brief update on "a day in the life" of your prospective customer.

Invite them to slip into this role as best they can. They need to imagine themselves actually "being" this person. Tell them you want to know how your value proposition sounds from this person's perspective. Have them close their eyes. Then, tell them your value proposition.

When you are done sharing it, ask, "As you sit in my prospect's shoes:

- how did my value proposition *sound?*"
- what caught your attention?"
- what was boring, weak, or unimportant?"

You must realize that it doesn't matter what you say; what matters is what your customer hears. If something isn't clicking, stop using it. If something piqued their interest, use it again!

Your value proposition is the foundation of everything we'll be focusing on in the rest of this book. If you want to get into big companies, it's imperative that you invest time in figuring out what your value proposition is and how to best articulate it.

KEY POINTS

- Conduct in-depth interviews with existing customers to discover the true value of your offering. They're your best source of information.
- Leverage the collective wisdom of your colleagues to help you define the value proposition inherent in your offering.
- To quantify business value, compare your customer's prior measurements to the results they attain after using your product or service; engage new customers in the process of creating meaningful metrics.
- When lacking client measurement, speak in business terminology and leverage industry statistics.
- Test your value proposition's effectiveness with existing or simulated customers prior to using it; modify it as needed.

8

KNOWING ENOUGH
TO GET IN

If you want big companies to be
your clients, you won't find any shortcuts. Your incredible charm, de-
lightful wit, or keen intelligence are simply not enough. To significantly
increase your likelihood of getting your foot in the door, immerse yourself in your targeted customer's business prior to initiating contact.

Often when I give workshops, I start out by asking people to share
their most memorable sales experience. Over the years, I've heard a lot
of great stories, but few have stuck in my memory more than Mike's experience in selling computer systems.

After months of calling, he'd finally landed an appointment with an
executive in a large corporation. Mike was pumped and cocky. He loved
meeting with senior-level people. At the beginning of their conversation, he focused the discussion on what was happening in the industry—
a deliberate strategy of his to warm things up. Then Mike casually said,
"So tell me about your company."

The executive looked at him stunned. Then he turned around and
started searching for something in his credenza. When he found it, he
swung his chair back to Mike. "Here," he said. "Read this. And when
you're done, come back and talk to me."

The executive then escorted Mike to a lobby down the hall, leaving him alone to read the company's annual report. Needless to say, Mike never got a second chance to talk to this man. Nor would anyone else who's not prepared. Most sellers don't even get this far if they haven't done their research.

In the new sales paradigm, knowledge is power. It separates the good sellers from the average ones and the committed from the complacent. If you don't invest time learning about an organization before getting in, corporate decision makers write you off as a lightweight. Having only a cursory knowledge of your targeted account's business is simply not enough.

DIG UP THE DIRT

Corporate decision makers today expect you to be conversant about their company and what's important to them. That's what they're interested in—not your product, service, or solution. They don't expect you to know all the gory details, just to be reasonably up-to-date on what's happening in their organization. With good precall research and analysis, you'll be able to:

- figure out how your product or service impacts your customer's business;
- have provocative discussions driven by the intelligent questions you ask;
- generate high-value ideas to improve their performance, cut costs, increase sales, or gain a competitive advantage;
- create an informed business strategy; and
- differentiate yourself from all the other sellers trying to get their foot in the door.

Doing this research helps you take the "cold" out of cold calls. You're prepared to talk to decision makers. You know who they are and what's important to them. You know the words they use to describe their business and the direction their company is headed. You're never shooting in the dark. It's a huge confidence boost.

When you target a major corporation, focus your initial research on these four areas:

1. Find a Point of Entry.   Because your primary goal is to get in, look for the easiest way to penetrate the account. That means you need to find business units or divisions within the company that seem like they could be a good fit for your offering. Review your target market definition before you begin this research.

My first project at 3M was in their business products division. I knew that my experience selling copiers would make me a credible resource. Yet there are entire business units within 3M where the fit is poor and my strengths bring little value. I've never called on the group that sells Post-It™ Notes and never will.

I have friends who own a marketing communications firm. Over the years, they've developed expertise in working with smaller medical technology firms. Should they decide to pursue business with 3M, they'd have a much greater shot at getting into their health care business unit than into the home and leisure products division.

Think "fit" all the time and you'll hone in much faster on the best point of entry into the big companies. Also, by ruling out certain business units, divisions, or departments, you don't waste time trying to get into places where the opportunities for success are limited.

2. Learn about Their Business.   The amount of time you invest researching and learning about a prospective client should be directly proportional to their value to your business.

If landing a contract with this big firm puts megabucks into your pocket, has high prestige value, or huge opportunities for growth, then it's worth spending lots of time on. Also, if what you're selling has a major organizational impact, it's essential to spend significantly more time in the research phase. For those types of accounts, you need to be conversant about your prospective customer's:

- Industry trends
- Business changes
- High priority initiatives
- Critical success factors
- Key business issues

- Financial drivers
- Product and service lines
- Competitors
- Key customers
- Primary decision makers

If your offering affects only a portion of the business (e.g., marketing, distribution, packaging, or manufacturing), you need to know much of the same information, but on a smaller scale. If the account isn't that valuable to you from a growth or referral perspective, then you put in less work as well.

> Need help understanding business terms and acronyms? Check out the Glossarist Web site. *http://www.glossarist.com/glossaries/business*

3. Search for Openings. As you research, keep your eyes and ears open for anything that hints that this particular account might be a solid prospect for you. Specifically, you'll want to look for these two things:

1. *Problem Indicators*—information that leads you to believe they're struggling with challenges and issues that you could resolve.
2. *Opportunity Indicators*—information that points to goals, objectives, or strategic imperatives that you can help them achieve or attain.

Before you begin, write down what these indicators are so that you know what you're looking for. Personally, I look for:

- how sales are tracking (stagnation is good; training may be needed).
- what's said about new product introductions potentially (a great opening for me).
- if their market is changing (new sales skills may be required for success).
- the need to expand the customer base (if getting in is tough; training may be needed).

If you've already honed in on your target market, these should be easy for you to identify. These are the enabling conditions we talked about earlier in Chapter 5.

4. Key in on the Lingo. The final thing you look for is the words that the company uses to describe their business, their problems, and their opportunities. Why? Because when you prepare your account entry strategy—which includes phone calls, letters, and more—you want to speak your customer's language. The closer your words mimic their language, the easier it is for you to get in.

When one of my clients was researching a targeted account, the client discovered that "operational efficiency" was plastered on everything they read. We made sure that we used that very same phrase in all our communications with the targeted account.

TAP INTO ONLINE RESOURCES

If you're already busy, where do you find the time to do all this research? You eliminate making all those stupid, nonresearched calls that have minimal or no payback. If you're like most people, this should free up lots of time. Then you focus only on the better opportunities where there's a good fit. The result? Less work yields more sales.

Scrutinize Their Web Site

The obvious place to start is at the company's Web site. First check out the various business units and product offerings. Take a good look at:

- *Company Overview:* Learn about the company profile, history, people and values, partners, community involvement, and more.
- *Investor Relations:* Download a copy of the annual report. Check out the latest 10k for detailed explanations of the business issues.
- *Press Room or Media Center:* Read the latest press releases to keep up-to-date on the latest happenings in the company. Listen to speeches by their executives.

- *People or Leadership:* If you're selling at the executive level, this is critical information. Learn as much as you can about those running the corporation prior to contacting them.
- *Site Map:* This can help you find other "hidden" information that doesn't readily appear on pages you're likely to frequent.

For very important accounts you can easily spend four to five or more hours reviewing this material and checking out other online resources. You don't have to go overboard for every account. Nor do you need to analyze their financial numbers in great depth unless this information is vital to your sales efforts. For me, this detailed analysis has never made a difference because I'm more interested in trends and commentary.

Basically, you want to be able to talk knowledgeably about the account and know what's important to them. This information helps to develop your account entry strategy and plan your meetings.

> As you research, keep asking, "How can my product or service make a difference for this customer?"

Dig Deep into a Resource Gold Mine

The Web is a veritable gold mine of information about companies. While this information is available to anyone who wants to tap into it, the vast majority of sellers barely leverage this incredible resource.

There's so much out there that sometimes you get lost searching for those golden nuggets of information. Rather than waste hours searching through a bunch of irrelevant sites filled with worthless drivel, check out these Web sites:

Corporate Information. *http://www.corporateinformation.com.* This site is full of detailed information on public companies. Registration is free, but required. When I typed in one prospect's name, I found 27 relevant articles supplied by industry analysts.

Edgar Scan. *http://www.edgarscan.pwcglobal.com.* Edgar Scan has incredible information on public companies, benchmarking capabilities, and great graphical displays.

Thomas Register. *http://www.thomasregister.com.* This site is full of information on manufacturers; it's great for identifying other firms similar to your best customers.

> For more online resources, see Appendix B and check out *http://www.sellingtobigcompanies.com.*

Did you know that only 20 percent of the information on the Internet is accessible through Google? That's right. The majority of information you might want to access is on the "hidden Web" housed on secure servers that companies pay high subscription fees to have access to.

That's wonderful if you work for a large corporation, but it leaves smaller businesses out in the cold. To get access to much of this information, visit your local library. If there is a research librarian on staff, this person can help you find what you're looking for. Some even let you access their subscription databases from your own computer. Another excellent resource is the James J. Hill Reference Library. For a very reasonable annual fee, they give small businesses online access to the same information that only big companies can typically afford. Their trade journal database is second to none.

GET CREATIVE TO GET THE SCOOP

Don't just look online, though. By being creative you can find numerous ways to learn more about what's happening inside your targeted account. Here are just a few of my favorite methods.

Interview Their Customers

What you learn from interviews with their customers is totally seductive to corporate decision makers. A business consultant I knew wanted to set up a meeting with an executive in a major printing firm. By snooping around, he identified some of their top local clients. He compiled a list of questions he knew would be of high interest to the decision maker. (They just happened to be highly relevant to his offering as well.) After the interviews were completed, he contacted the executive and got right in.

Talk with People Who Work There

Sometimes you learn invaluable information just by talking to people who work at the company. My neighbor works at a large technology firm. At a neighborhood party he shared some info about the long hours he was working and the challenges the company was facing. What he said wasn't confidential, but it was one of my *problem indicators.* I was able to leverage this knowledge to get an appointment in a completely different division. If you get creative, you'll find numerous opportunities to interact with someone who works for any company.

Order or Use Their Products or Services

Depending on your offering, you could learn an incredible amount by ordering or using a target account's products or services. You could evaluate quality, the delivery process, customer service, return procedures, packaging, and more. You could compare the information with other suppliers' information to see how they stack up against their competition. You could identify problems or opportunities for improvement.

Visit a Trade Show

This method proved extremely valuable to me in getting into one of my clients. I attended a local technology trade show to find some new prospects. Many big companies were exhibiting, and I talked with lots of people. At one firm's booth (an ideal client) I had long discussions with several of their salespeople. We talked about their new products, changing marketplace direction, and sales challenges. One sales representative even gave me the names, e-mails, and phone numbers of all the people I needed to contact.

As you can see, there is an endless supply of ways to get good quality information about a big company you target. Request their marketing materials. Talk to their competitors. Interview the executives for an article you're writing. Ask their executives to speak to an organization to which you belong. Over the years, I've done all these things—especially when I have my eyes set on getting into a very specific account that could be extremely lucrative for me. These techniques work, and they're fun to do.

WATCH FOR TRIGGERING EVENTS

Alert! Alert! Once you identify the big companies you want to target, your job is to keep on top of what's happening in their business. You're looking for *triggering events*—those changes in their organization or in the outside world that can create openings for your products, services, or solutions.

What should you be on the lookout for? These newsworthy events can create just the opportunity you need to get your foot in the door:

- Poor quarterly earnings or annual results
- Recent spin-offs, mergers, or acquisitions
- New funding received
- Important new product or service announcements
- Expansion into new market segments or geographical areas
- Downsizing or rightsizing
- Restructurings and reorganizations
- New management or ownership
- Pending or recently enacted legislation
- Resignations or additions of key personnel
- Downward spiral in business
- Landing a prestigious new client
- National or international events and crises
- Availability of new technology

Triggering events create a "ripple effect" through the entire organization. If you haven't explored this technique yet, you might want to ask yourself, "How might these events create a need for my product or service?" These *triggering events* are a critical reason why big companies may suddenly be more receptive to your offering.

For example, if your targeted account announces an acquisition, tons of sales opportunities are created. Computer systems need to be integrated. Supply chains are reevaluated. Sales forces are merged; employees are let go. Marketing collateral needs to be redesigned. Teamwork and collaboration are necessary as people jockey for position. Existing suppliers may have to reestablish their value.

One of my clients, an entrepreneurial professional services firm, keeps a keen eye on legislation. When new laws are pending or have just been passed, they leverage the news to get themselves in to meet with key decision makers from competitive accounts. In the past year, they experienced significant growth using this strategy.

Because *triggering events* signal a potential ripeness for your product or services, it's important to keep abreast of what's going on in your targeted accounts. If they're in your own backyard, you can scan the business pages of your local newspaper. You can also keep up-to-date on what's happening by:

- signing up at various Web sites (e.g., *http://www.bizjournal.com, http://www.yahoo.com*) to be notified when announcements are made about the big companies you're following;
- reading trade journals or attending association meetings focused on the industry segment your targeted client is in; and
- signing up at Google News or Yahoo! News to receive notification of their latest press releases (*http://news.google.com* and *http://news.yahoo.com*).

Fortunately (and somewhat surprisingly) most sellers don't think like this, so you may be alone in using *triggering events* as a strategy to get your foot in the door. That's good! If the competition doesn't capitalize on these events, your position is that much stronger. Best of all, focusing your sales efforts on companies who are highly receptive to your offering both shortens and simplifies your sales process.

KEY POINTS

- Corporate decision makers expect you to be conversant about their company and business. That's what they're interested in—not your product or service.

- Use your precall research to find a *good point of entry* into a large corporation, as well as to identify *problem indicators* and *opportunity indicators.*
- Leverage multiple venues (e.g., online resources, customer interviews, employee conversations, trade shows) to learn about your prospective customer's business, needs, issues, and challenges.
- Watch for *triggering events* to create significant opportunities for you to get your foot in the door.
- The amount of time you spend learning about prospective customers should be directly proportional to their potential value to you.

Chapter

9

LEVERAGE YOUR NETWORK

Setting up meetings from a cold call is a challenge; no one owes you the favor of meeting with them. That's the harsh truth. That's why so many people are out networking these days. They're looking to establish relationships with prospective buyers first as a foot-in-the-door strategy.

And referrals—ooh, how we dream of having someone put in a good word for us with a person who works at a big company. With a referral, it's so much easier to set up meetings with corporate decision makers. The very best referrals come from coworkers or peers inside the company. After that, referrals from trusted industry colleagues are great door openers. Without a referral, everything in sales is just that much harder.

After refocusing my business several years ago, I hit the networking circuit to find some new clients. Like everyone, I believed the standard wisdom about the value of networking. Because I'm not a shy, tongue-tied person, I figured networking would be a snap. All I needed to do was observe these guidelines from Networking 101:

- Focus on the other person.
- Ask lots of questions to make them feel important.

- Share ideas and resources to help them achieve their objectives.
- Keep in touch so you won't be quickly forgotten.

For many months I was one busy person. I attended a variety of networking events: after-hour socials, breakfast gatherings, and luncheon meetings. I joined several organizations that were closely tied to my business, got involved on committees, helped out during monthly meetings, and hosted trade show booths. I was even the featured speaker at some of these events.

Yet I never saw the results I was hoping for. In fact, I barely saw any positive results for all the time I invested in networking.

WHY MOST NETWORKING IS A WASTE OF TIME

For a long time I was stymied. Finally it hit me! Most everything I'd learned about networking wasn't true in today's business climate. Here are the three biggest myths I uncovered.

Myth 1

Local business organizations and professional associations are great places to meet prospective customers.

Reality. This is absolutely false if you're targeting big companies. Most people who attend these networking functions are from small-sized to medium-sized businesses. You seldom, if ever, meet decision makers from General Mills, General Electric, or General Dynamics because they're too swamped to come. Should they happen to show up, vendors converging on them from all angles force them to put up a defensive screen.

People who work for big companies do network—just not at the community level. They prefer to meet with their counterparts from other divisions or to attend industry-specific events and trade shows.

Myth 2

People you meet at networking events gladly refer you to their contacts in large corporations.

Reality. Most people you meet at networking meetings are really nice but may be even hungrier than you are for business. They're desperately hoping to meet someone who will give them a great referral into that elusive corporate decision maker.

But let's get real. Would you introduce someone you just met to your corporate clients? I sure wouldn't. When someone uses my name as a referral source, it implies that I've put my stamp of approval on him or her. Until I have a better sense of this person's capabilities, character, values, style, and more, I will not risk my good name! Nobody would when their personal reputation and ultimately their financial well-being is at stake.

Myth 3

Because it takes time to see the results of your networking efforts, keep at it.

Reality. Yes, it does take a while to see networking results. But if the big company decision makers aren't there—and won't be coming—then you're wasting your time. The longer you keep at it, the more time you're wasting. Using traditional networking strategies and venues to get into large corporations takes forever. You could go broke first. Get off your butt and stop hoping that networking will get you into big companies. It takes a far more proactive approach in today's marketplace.

BUILD YOUR NETWORKING FOUNDATION

Successful networking doesn't happen serendipitously. You must be deliberate about it. As you develop your strategy, keep in mind the two primary purposes of networking:

1. Finding the right people to help you get into an account.
2. Finding people who have information that will get you to the next step in your account entry strategy, whatever that might be.

In order for others to help you out, you need to be crystal clear with them about your target market, the problems your decision makers are encountering, or the goals they want to achieve. This is when you use your elevator speech, that one-sentence to two-sentence statement that answers the question, "What do you do?"

It should be so clear that when people hear your elevator speech they say, "You need to meet Terry. She was complaining about that exact issue last time we talked." Or else they say, "I have to introduce you to Bryan. That's what he's trying to accomplish in his division."

Elevator speeches are less specific than your value proposition but share the essence of what you're doing. They overtly state the type of customer you work with so your fellow networkers know when someone would be an ideal prospect for you.

Use a Problem-Centered Approach

Because issues and challenges typically have top-of-mind awareness, problem-centered elevator speeches are generally more effective. Here's a formula you can use to create a problem-centered elevator speech:

"I/we work with (insert target market) . . . who are (insert feeling word) . . . with (insert problem/issue you solve)."

One of my good friends is an organizational development consultant. She used to say, "I do team building." Now she uses this elevator speech: "I help fragmented leadership teams who are struggling with communication issues and turf wars." It's been much more effective for her.

Use a Benefit-Centered Approach

These elevator speeches are focused on what customers want to achieve. There's a gap between their current reality and their desired future state. Here's a formula you can use to create a benefit-centered elevator speech:

> "I/we work with/help (target market) . . . who want to (describe what your customers want)."

When I first started coaching a software sales representative, his elevator speech was, "We sell and implement fully-integrated CRM systems compatible with all the major data base applications utilized by the Fortune 500."

What a mouthful! I'm sure his marketing people would have been proud of him for using the company line so accurately—even if it never worked. He got much better results when he changed to: "We help large companies use their customer information to drive repeat sales and reduce customer turnover."

Focus on Specific Opportunities

When you attend a networking event, go with a clear picture in mind of whom you'd like to set up an appointment with. This significantly increases the success of your networking efforts. Be prepared to tell people what company you want to get into and the title of the person you'd like to see:

> "I'd really like to meet a marketing director from the Group Sales division of Prudential."

> "You wouldn't happen to know anyone who works in the information technology area of the Commercial Aviation Services business at Boeing?"

The person you're networking with may or may not know someone who fits the parameters you describe. But they may know someone who knows—and that's valuable too. Sometimes you just need one connection to get started.

MAXIMIZE YOUR BUSINESS CONNECTIONS

Because people from big companies rarely attend local networking events, what can you do? How can you leverage your network to get your foot in the door? Don't wait for serendipity to happen.

Springboard from Existing Contacts

Several months ago I decided to chronicle my attempts to get into one of my targeted accounts on my blog. Because I didn't know anyone who worked there, I felt it would be a great case study. I mentioned the idea to a few colleagues. Believe it or not, within a week I had the names of two excellent management contacts in their sales organization. That's why it's so important to let your contacts know whom you want to meet. Be very explicit and you'll be amazed at what you uncover.

Here are several strategies that other creative networkers have used:

- A woman in the construction industry regularly meets with other salespeople in related markets. She handpicked the group with care; they're all vendors she respects. With their combined network, she can easily get connected to decision makers in big companies.
- A new manufacturing sales representative set up one-on-one meetings with several salespeople in his distribution channel. Through these contacts he is quickly networked into the corporate decision makers with whom he needs to meet.
- The owner of an event planning service is constantly on the lookout for new opportunities. He routinely leverages his college alumni network to get into his targeted accounts across the country. The group has an online board for just this type of networking.

Institutionalize Your Networking

Some companies have institutionalized networking to minimize the need to "cold call" and to increase their chances of getting referred in by a respected colleague or friend. They routinely circulate company names looking for possible connections. It's a very deliberate and effective networking strategy.

Bruce Malmgren is Vice President of Client Resources at Right Management Consulting, a career transition and organizational consulting firm. People in his business live and die by networking that's focused on finding contacts at very specific targeted companies.

"In our office, on a monthly basis, each salesperson names one company they want to network their way into," says Bruce. "We publish this list internally. And, we ask our clients, friends, or anyone else we're comfortable with about people they might know in this organization."

Go Where Your Decision Makers Go

So where are you most likely to find those prospective corporate clients? Conferences and trade shows in their particular market or industry segment are your best bets. These functions cost more to attend and frequently require travel, but the payback is often well worth it.

"My ideal client is a specialty retail chain, so last year I attended the national retail conference," said business development consultant Kelley Robertson. "I made a few contacts, and one of them turned into a lucrative account. Since then, I've stopped going to 'typical' networking events. Right now I'm on track to double my business this year!"

CREATE OPPORTUNITIES WITH STRATEGIC ALLIANCES

Strategic alliances are the most powerful networking strategy I've ever used. Big companies often arrange them at the corporate level, but anyone can create his or her own network of strategic partners. A single salesperson can easily form an alliance that catapults his or her business to the next level. Small businesses, professional services firms, and independent consultants can easily leverage their relationship with alliance partners to expand their opportunities too.

A strategic alliance is *not* a merger of your businesses. It's simply a go-to-market method that extends your reach far beyond what you're capable of reaching on your own. Each participant brings his and her own expertise, knowledge of the market, and client relationships to the alliance.

Together you figure out how to leverage your unique combination of businesses and talent to (1) help your mutual clients achieve their goals and (2) grow your own sales.

The best partners for a successful strategic alliance are businesses with related specialties to yours and firms that sell to the same decision makers. Here are two examples of alliances that turned out to be extremely profitable for all involved:

1. A division of one of my corporate clients sells sandpaper and tape to the automotive industry. Their top-selling representative independently established an informal strategic alliance with other vendors selling to the painting area. By keeping on top of new developments, he ensures that his customers don't experience any line-stopping problems. He's now so valuable to the client that lower-cost competitors can't displace him.

2. Over the past several years, I've joined forces with other companies involved in new product launches to put on a joint seminar. We each talk on our areas of expertise. I focus on the hand-off of the new product to the sales organization, while others speak on lead generation, marketing, research, and branding. We co-market the event to our combined databases of clients. The event pays for itself, but most importantly everyone nets new clients.

Find Good Partners

First of all, ask yourself, "Who do I know today that's in a business contiguous to mine?" and "Who else has the same target market as I do and sells to my primary decision maker?" You just need one other person to get started down this path. Look for others who are doing well, have big company clients already, and want to grow. I strongly recommend that you avoid setting up an alliance with someone who is desperate for business. The time you invest in figuring out how to work with each other actually saps your *oomph* and derails your sales efforts.

Get to Know Each Other First

You need to invest time up front to really understand each other's products or services. When you bring in someone else, you need to have confidence in this person's ability to do the work, take care of the account, and act ethically. Don't rush this process or you may be sorry. I've seen people blindly trust their "partners" only to find out later that it was a huge mistake.

Pick One Project to Work On at First

Start out by dating—you don't need to get married right away. Our first venture was a joint seminar. There wasn't a lot of risk because we weren't bringing each other into our best clients. It was also a good chance for us to see each other in action. In doing the seminar, we divvied up the work according to our expertise. The event went smoothly. We all heard each other speak and present. It was a good opportunity to assess each other's abilities at a deeper level and to build trust.

Expand the Relationship

Once you're comfortable that you want to work with your strategic alliance partner on an ongoing basis, explore ways to take your relationship to the next level. Here is what's happened with my partners:

- We confidently bring each other in to meet our clients.
- We brainstorm how best to work with our mutual clients. By pooling our knowledge we're able to come up with much better solutions for them.
- We co-market each other's business in multiple ways: referrals, e-newsletters, Web sites, blogs, and more.

These ideas just tap the surface of what can be done with strategic alliances. If you're still trying to go it alone out there, consider forming a strategic alliance with other firms. If you choose the right partners, it will make a huge difference in your business.

KEY POINTS

- Traditional networking venues are a waste of time if you're looking for corporate decision makers; they don't attend.
- Elevator speeches that clearly define your target market and what they're struggling with help potential referrers point you in the right direction.
- Let your existing business contacts know which firms you've targeted and who you're trying to reach; they're frequently a wealth of untapped information.
- For maximum impact, leverage strategic alliances to expand your business opportunities into the corporate marketplace.
- Today's marketplace requires a much more active, creative, and deliberate approach to networking if you want to make it easier to get your foot in the door of large corporations.

Part Three

LAUNCH THE CAMPAIGN

10

IDENTIFY KEY DECISION MAKERS

"**W**ho do I call on?" It's highly likely that this question is at the forefront of your mind right now. I hear it all the time and wish I could give you a simple answer. The truth is that it's a challenge to find out who makes decisions. Stringent security policies keep you out of big companies unless you know who you're meeting. This puts you in a real conundrum if you don't know a soul who works there.

Several years ago I decided it was time to do business with a local high-tech firm. My only connection to the company was the ex-wife of a former neighbor. We hadn't spoken in at least three years, but I called her anyway to explain my dilemma. She didn't know who I should speak to, but she put me in touch with three colleagues she thought might be able to help. I called all three, got voice mail, and left them messages. Two called back. When I explained who I was looking for, they referred me to their connections.

All told, it took seven calls spread over a week for me to identify the right decision maker. The total time invested—less than 30 minutes. So while it may seem like a lot of work, it isn't. You just have to make the calls.

DEFINE THE ELUSIVE DECISION MAKER

With so many possible entry points into a big company, many sellers make the mistake of going to the purchasing or human resources (HR) departments first. This is a fatal error. Let me repeat that. This is a fatal error.

The purchasing folks are looking for the best possible pricing for a very specific solution. Despite all your best efforts to bring value and be consultative, they will force you into competing on price alone. Avoid calling HR folks too—unless what you're offering specifically impacts their area. They generally have minimal influence on decisions outside their department. They're often out of touch with the business problems facing the organization. While they may be interested in your offering, don't count on them to promote it to the people they serve. They have good intentions, but little power.

In researching your targeted accounts, you may have discovered the names of potential decision makers. But with the constant reorganization in companies today, it's tough to find the right person on your first attempt—especially if they're hidden deep in the bowels of the corporation.

To keep your sanity during this information-gathering phase of your "getting in" campaign, approach it as a game. Imagine that you're searching for the main character in the book *Where's Waldo?* or picture yourself as a detective trying to discover "whodunit."

Because you'll be engaging others in your search for these elusive people, it's imperative to be able to clearly describe the people with whom you'd like to meet. This can be done by explaining the following about them:

- *Position:* This is often the most common way of locating a decision maker because it's how companies label their personnel. Yet the closer you get to the decision maker, the more internal resistance it generates as people want to protect their peers from time-wasting sellers.
- *Responsibility:* Sometimes it's easier to find people by what they're in charge of rather than by their job titles. Examples could be "the person responsible for warehouse design in your supply chain area" or "the individual who makes decisions on plastics suppliers in Chicago."

- *Problem or Goal:* You're looking for the person or group that's wrestling with one of the company's key business initiatives. For example, you might ask: "Where would I find the people who are concerned about shortening time-to-profitability on new product introductions?" or "Who is involved in the group that's evaluating price optimization strategies for the retail markets?" (This is my favorite because it's business focused and prevents you from hearing the "We're not interested" response. I use it when I'm getting close to where decisions are actually being made.)

Remember this major caveat: When you're searching for names, don't sell—not even one little bit. Keep in the information-gathering mode. You'll have ample opportunity to sell in the near future!

Use Telephone Strategies to Find the Right Names

The phone is your best tool for finding corporate decision makers' names. It's fast. It's proactive. You build momentum each time you uncover a name that puts you closer to your prospective buyer. Plus, by asking questions of each person you talk to, you learn more about what's happening in their business that's relevant to your offering.

Start with the phone company. This simple but often overlooked technique can provide you with myriad options. Call directory assistance and get a listing of all the local phone numbers—not just the main corporate number. You can get the numbers to your targeted firm's research facilities, manufacturing plants, human resources, accounts receivable, retail outlets, sales offices, technical support, customer service, and so on.

Try calling any of these different locations for assistance. Because employees from these offices seldom get these calls, they're much less averse to giving out names. In fact, they can help you find some pretty good contacts. Ask them to transfer you if at all possible. Also see if you can get the person's direct-dial number or e-mail address. This is to your benefit, because busy corporate employees check caller ID prior to picking up the phone. Calls coming from the main switchboard are frequently rolled right into voice mail because the likelihood of them being from a salesperson is high.

If you contact the primary corporate number, the people who answer the phones want to help you out. They're *not* gatekeepers trying to protect "the boss" from interruptions. Realize that they may be constrained by a corporate policy that prohibits them from giving out names or direct-dial numbers.

If you tell switchboard operators the name of the position you're trying to reach and in what area of their company, they'll do their best to help out. You might say:

> "I'd like to speak to the Chief Technology Officer of the Humanics division."

> "Could you put me through to the HR Director with Industrial Markets?"

Because big companies are so geographically dispersed and have so many employees, it's highly likely that switchboard operators won't know who to connect you with. If that happens, suggest they put you through to someone in the division, department, or business unit. This gets you one step closer to finding the right names. Other strategies that have proven effective include these:

- Contact a salesperson who works for the division you'd like to get into. Sellers have great empathy for your situation and are often very willing to help out.
- Call the highest-level person you can find in the specific area of the company you're trying to reach. You'll likely end up reaching an administrative assistant. Explain your needs briefly and ask to be redirected to the appropriate person.
- Go to the "Contact Us" page on their Web site to find a number for an actual person who's willing to help you out. While you're there, fill out the online form to see if you can get someone to tell you who's in charge of the functional area within the specific division you want to work with.
- Start with a smaller, local office of the big company—even if it's not in your backyard. They're often more willing to help you out than large corporate offices.

PIGGYBACK OFF THE NAMES YOU UNCOVER

When making these information-gathering calls, I suggest starting with a factual no-nonsense, professional approach. You're calling to get a name, that's all. One step at a time, you move closer and closer to the actual decision maker. Each time you talk with someone new you have a chance to add to your knowledge pool.

Again, there's no selling involved. Simply state your name and company, although that's even optional. Tell the people you reach that you need their help. If you tell them the position you'd like to reach and they're stuck, offer alternatives. For example, if the person I talked to couldn't find the vice president of sales, I could suggest they look for these titles as well: chief sales officer, national sales manager, director of sales, or head of their sales organization.

Get the Basics

No matter whom you're talking to, it's imperative to get some basic information before being transferred. In *Cold Calling for Women,* Wendy Weiss suggests you use these magic words: "Before you connect me (pause), I need to reach (give title). Who is that, please?"

Speaking from experience, I can assure you that this phrase will save you from much embarrassment. More than once I've been sent to the right buyer but didn't have a clue who she or he was. Now, if at all possible, I always get the following information right away:

- The person's full name
- Its correct spelling
- A direct-dial number
- An e-mail address

That way, if I'm routed to voice mail—which is highly likely—I'll be able to contact this person at a later time. I also make sure to get the referrer's full name too because I'll need it in my follow-up calls.

Follow Up on the Connections

Whether the names you're following up with come from a network connection, the switchboard, or accounts payable, you'll probably run smack dab into voice mail again.

The person you're trying to reach is busy and you're a stranger who wants some of their time. They won't call you back unless you give them a bona fide reason to do so. The key to getting callbacks is twofold: (1) you must include the referrer's name and (2) you need to pique their interest.

I recommend leaving a voice mail such as this:

> "Terry. This is Jane Conrad from SureFire! Consulting. I just spoke with Maria Gonzalez in Customer Service. She said you were the person I needed to talk to get my question answered. Could you please give me a call? I'll be in my office later this afternoon. My number is . . . "

Would it make you curious? Most people wonder what it's all about and give you a quick call back. Everything you said is absolutely true. Never, ever lie to someone. But think about what it would take to break through all the clutter on their desk and in their minds. You can't just leave a bland, boring message and expect someone to call you back.

If you don't get a return call, try again. Rome wasn't conquered in a day. Neither are big companies. Also, be prepared to make multiple contacts to identify the exact person you need to see. Don't get discouraged if you run into dead ends initially. Just keep at it.

As you become more comfortable calling into big companies, over time you may develop a fun, offbeat approach that catches people off-guard. In my voice mail or when I get someone on the line, with a bit of jest I just might say:

> "Hey Bob. Jill Konrath calling. I hear you're the Go-To Guy (Big Kahuna) in your company. Sally Smith from your local sales office says you know everything! I have a quick question and I'm stumped. Please, please can you help me!"

Humor works. It's a breath of fresh, relaxing air in a high-stress environment. Customers embrace it; they want to talk with you and are more open to helping you out. But use humor only if it suits your personality and you're comfortable with that tone. Don't force it, or it could work against you. For most sellers, it's easier to stay in the mode of an information-gathering researcher at first. That's totally fine.

EMPLOY INTERNET STRATEGIES TO IDENTIFY DECISION MAKERS

The Internet is full of resources to help you identify the names you're looking for. Sam Richter, president of the nonprofit James J. Hill Reference Library, a resource for publicly accessible business information, shared these ideas.

- Search the Internet site of the targeted business unit or division of a big company. It's often hard to find within the corporate site. To locate it, use Google. Enter the company name in quotes followed by "AND" or "+" and then the division name in quotes. Example: "General Mills" AND "Food Service." Extend this search by adding parameters such as job titles, products, or a person's name.
- Check out *Business Journal*'s Web site (see Appendix B for its address). First decide if you want to search for news by industry or by market (New York, Atlanta). Then enter your search parameters just as you did with Google.
- Take a look at local papers; they're great resources for finding names. Newslink's Web site gives you access to media outlets around the world.
- Research trade journals. They carry articles written by people deep within the corporate hierarchy. Check with your local research librarian for help. FindArticles is the best open-source resource for this.

Explore Online Communities

Online communities are emerging resources that can help you make your initial connections into big companies. They're based on the principle that we're all within six degrees of separation from the exact person we'd like to meet—but we just don't know it.

Spoke and LinkedIn are two of the leading online communities today. They work by connecting people through protected referral chains. If you're a member of these communities, you can search for connections to specific companies, people, and positions. When you identify someone you're interested in meeting, you initiate a request for connection. The individual who's the referral source can then decide if he or she will allow it to happen.

This technology is also available for corporations to use behind their firewalls. It enables them to capitalize on their organization's "relationship capital" by creating a network of who-knows-whom across an entire enterprise.

Sellers who leverage these online communities report an increased response rate and shortened sales cycles when they contact prospective customers. This happens because they were "referred" by a trusted resource of the decision maker.

Ryze and Ecademy are more social types of business networks where you can talk with others who have similar interests. Through these online communities you can establish personal relationships with people who might be willing, once they know you, to put you in touch with their corporate contacts.

A word of caution: Don't expect the networks to do the hard work for you. Phone calls still need to be made, but your cold calls are now a little warmer.

Investigate Online Contact Locators

Business contact marketplaces are the newest online resource for sellers. Jigsaw is the first to launch this exciting service where people can buy, sell, and trade contact information. Community members have access to a continually growing database of fresh and accurate information on corporate decision makers.

Jigsaw is a collaborative system with each member providing a few pieces to the puzzle that Jigsaw then assembles for the benefit of the entire community. In short, by inputting the information (name, title, address, phone, e-mail, fax) on one of your contact's business cards, you get access to a certain number of other contacts in the database. You can conduct searches across companies or within companies. Your search can be refined even further by selecting criteria such as department, job title, or ZIP code. The more names you enter, the more withdrawals you get to make. If you don't want to provide contact information, you just pay a monthly fee for the service.

As the use of these types of resources grow, the databases will be even more valuable. Sellers won't have to sift through tons of material to find the right person. Nor will they have to make as many phone calls. The headaches involved in locating corporate contacts will be minimal.

If these online resources are new to you, I strongly suggest you check into them because this technology holds much potential. Some sellers are already reaping impressive results from using them. Appendix B provides links to many of these online resources.

KEY POINTS

- Your own clarity in defining the decision maker you want to reach is essential for the best results. Use the following parameters in your definition: position, responsibility, problem, or goal.
- If at all possible, avoid contacting the human resources or purchasing departments. Decisions are typically made elsewhere in the organization and implemented by these price-sensitive groups.
- When you're contacting companies to locate decision makers' names, don't sell. Keep yourself in the information-gathering mode.
- The phone is your most productive tool for finding decision makers buried inside a corporation. Plus you can uncover lots of valuable information as you conduct your search.
- Online communities and contact locators are fast emerging as invaluable resources for uncovering initial connections in a big company.

C h a p t e r

11

STOP WAITING FOR DECISION MAKERS TO CALL YOU BACK

It takes a while to locate decision makers in big companies. So when you finally hone in on just the right person, you're more than ready to get together. But you're also probably filled with tons of angst.

Wanting to sound professional but not anxious or overeager, you wrestle to find just the right words to say to this decision maker. Screw up what you say and you've blown your big chance. Nothing could be worse, especially because you invested so much time and effort to get to this point.

When you finally can't avoid this onerous task any longer, you pick up the phone and call. Of course you end up getting voice mail. So you blurt out your message the best you can, all the while thinking, "I hate prostituting myself like this. It feels like I'm begging."

Then you wait. And wait. But nobody calls you back. Doubt begins creeping in. You start thinking, "I'll never get in. Why would they want to work with me anyway?"

Perhaps you silently curse those rude people who work for big companies; if they had any manners at all, they'd return your phone calls. After all, you were respectful and pleasant to them. Maybe you blame your own company too for its poor marketing, ineffective lead generation efforts, or lack of advertising.

How long has it been since you left that message? A week now? Two weeks? Well, you can stop holding your breath right now because the chances that you'll get a return call from the decision maker are slim to none.

It doesn't matter that you spent countless hours researching the company, crafting a powerful value proposition and agonizing over the exact words you'd use in your message. It doesn't matter if a friend or colleague referred you.

The person you're trying to reach is swamped. Your phone call was just another unwanted interruption in an already overloaded day. So what can you do to penetrate their consciousness and show up on their radar screen?

WHY YOU NEED AN ACCOUNT ENTRY CAMPAIGN

To get into a big company today, you need to put together a strong account entry campaign from the very start. A single call just isn't enough.

You need to plan on seven to ten contacts before you get your foot in the door. This doesn't mean calling someone and leaving the exact same message every single time. If that's your approach, you'll be perceived as an irritating pest and never get a meeting.

Instead, you craft a multifaceted campaign that includes phone calls, e-mails, mailings, and faxes. Use your research on the big company as your starting point. As you plan your campaign, review what you've learned about their:

- goals and objectives,
- strategic business imperatives, and
- critical issues and challenges.

Analyze this information to determine the difference you can make. Think about results you've achieved with similar companies who used your product or service. Think about all the different ways you can help this company solve their problems and get to where they want to be. Then figure out how you can customize your value proposition so it is extremely tempting to the person you're calling.

> The key to a strong account entry campaign is to strategically share the value of working with you over multiple contacts.

Don't dump all your "goodies" on the table the first time you contact someone. You may think it really impresses them, but in reality they become overwhelmed and shut down. Worse yet, you don't have a good reason to get back with them anymore.

BREAK THROUGH THE MARKETING CLUTTER

Despite the fact that you've invested hours thinking about this particular decision maker, he or she has not spent one single solitary moment thinking about you. From his or her perspective, you don't exist. You're a voice mail that's easily deleted and immediately forgotten. To change this response, two things have to happen:

1. You need to carefully craft a variety of sales tools that focus on how you help your prospect's business.
2. You need to develop a well-planned account entry campaign to roll out your customer-centric messages.

Believe it or not, one of the best things about this process is that it takes the pressure off because you don't expect yourself to get immediate results. Instead, you know that you're establishing a relationship over time that demonstrates your value to their business. As you plan the campaign, focus on how to provide value and service, not "how to sell something today." This is how people who are successful selling to big companies think. Remember, decision makers could care less about your product or service—only the difference it can make!

In the last chapter, I shared how it took me seven phone calls to locate the decision maker in a local high-tech firm. Once I found his name, it took me another eight contacts to finally connect with him. Here's what happened over a two-month period.

Contact	Action Taken in Account Entry Campaign
1	Left a voice mail highlighting value proposition #1 related to new product introductions.
2	Sent letter focused on new product launch issues and relevant customer results.
3	Followed up via phone; left voice mail stressing different aspect of value proposition.
4	Faxed funny cartoon illustrating the "problem" with a brief note attached.
5	Left voice mail reiterating need to get together to discuss how to ensure successful launch on critical new product coming to market.
6	Talked to assistant. Found out the decision maker was out all week traveling but would be in Friday. Got e-mail and sent short message that I looked forward to talking with him soon.
7	Called on Friday at recommended time. Got voice mail and transferred to assistant. His schedule had changed and he was traveling. Got cell phone number.
8	Called cell phone and immediately reached decision maker in airport. Had short conversation, answered questions, and was referred to product marketing manager with blessings.

The result? I talked with the woman in product marketing the following week, set up a meeting, wrote a proposal, and had a very nice-sized contract within a month. No competitive bids were taken, and no one tried to knock my price down.

This all came about because of my precall research on the company. I discovered that the success of new products was critical to their financials in the upcoming year. Because I've worked on launches for years, I knew all the typical problems that sales organizations run into and how to alleviate them.

My entire account entry campaign was focused on this very critical business issue and was entirely personalized to the company's specific situation. I was determined to get their business because I knew I could make a difference.

Sound like a lot of work? It is at first because it requires a change in your mindset and requires that you plan out your various approaches in advance. But if you look at the amount of time it actually takes for each contact, it isn't a lot. Plus the upside potential can be extremely lucrative, especially if your initial contract turns into a long-term, highly profitable business relationship.

PACK YOUR CAMPAIGN TOOL KIT

Your tool kit will be as unique as you and your business. But what you won't find in it are brochures, catalogs, and the typical collateral produced en masse by marketing. Because all that stuff ends up in the wastebasket, there's absolutely no sense in using it. Not only do you waste your time and your money, but you also annoy decision makers. They see you as just another self-serving salesperson—which is absolutely the last way you want to be perceived.

What goes into your tool kit? Whatever you determine will break through all the marketing clutter and help your company name be recognized. Everything in your tool kit should focus on the business value you provide and build your credibility as an expert. Critical, must-have items for your tool kit include:

- Voice mail scripts with multiple iterations of your value proposition
- Telephone scripts for talking to an actual person
- Obstacle handling guides for dealing with the common objections you encounter
- Strong letters highlighting your primary value propositions as they relate to your targeted customer

These are the basics—the "don't leave home without them" items. The following chapters will deal with each of them in more depth.

Because you need multiple contacts in your account entry campaign, it's a good idea to have more items in your tool kit. Here are some ideas that have proven effective for others:

- *Success stories.* Decision makers are always interested in how other companies tackle the same challenges they're facing. Be sure to focus on the business results your customer attained.
- *White papers, special reports, and tips booklets.* Make sure these documents are highly informative or educational in nature. Well-written ones significantly enhance your credibility.
- *Relevant articles.* Whenever you find an article you think would be of interest to your prospect, send it off with a quick note: "I thought of you when I read this."
- *Invitations.* This is one of the best ways to get decision makers to check you out, especially if they don't have to leave their office. Offering information-rich teleseminars, Webcasts, or even formal seminars positions your company as a thought leader in your industry.
- *Newsletters.* Company newsletters with useful content add to your perceived expertise. Sent regularly, they're a highly effective keep-in-touch strategy. Make sure they're not brochures in disguise.
- *Books.* Have you read a good business book lately? If it's relevant to your prospects, buy another copy and send it off with a personal note. It can be a small investment with high payback.
- *Precontact referral letter.* Would one of your customers in a related industry be willing to send a letter on your behalf? If so, help him or her write it. A referral letter like this can work extremely well, especially if the people know each other.
- *Gift baskets.* The door-opening results achieved by sellers who use gift baskets can be an excellent investment for those corporate prospects you really want to work with.
- *Free samples.* If you can do this with your offering, definitely consider it as part of your account entry campaign. Be careful, though, that you don't give too much away. You still want to meet with the decision maker.
- *Postcards.* Postcards are always read. If you send postcards that contain tips or valuable information, people will keep them. Humorous ones get posted in their workspace too.

Please notice, handwritten notes and cards are not part of your account entry tool kit. They're relationship-building gestures that are "nice" but don't open the doors of the corporate decision maker. They work better after you get in.

Also, many of these items in your tool kit can be delivered via multiple mediums. They can be sent in a letter, e-mailed, faxed, sent by private delivery service such as FedEx, couriered, or delivered by hand. In your account entry campaign, you want to use a variety of methods to keep your message fresh.

IMPLEMENT YOUR ACCOUNT ENTRY CAMPAIGN

How does your campaign all flow together? Truthfully, there's no right or wrong way to make it happen. You can start with a phone call, a letter, or an e-mail. It doesn't matter. What counts is that your value proposition is conveyed in such an enticing manner that, after a few contacts, your prospects want to clear their schedule to meet with you.

Study This Campaign Case Study

Terry was in charge of business development for a small interactive advertising agency. Because the firm didn't have deep pockets, they had to rely on themselves to drive new business. Terry had these two goals for her account entry campaign:

1. Increase name recognition
2. Create a feeling of confidence

To start with, she created a nine-touch program that began with either a phone call or a letter. If she sent a letter, it focused on a current event at the prospect's company and how doing business with her firm could improve the result. The letter was hand-addressed and sent first class or FedExed to increase the chances of being opened.

In the letter Terry committed to following up at a specific date and time, which she always did. Yet nine out of ten times she was sent to voice mail, where she left a compelling message that ended with a request to talk. About two weeks later she followed up with an interesting article, sample proposal, or white paper sent in a mailing tube (because mailing tubes get opened faster than envelopes). Then she contacted the prospect by phone again.

Over the course of the next 12 weeks Terry identified six additional ways to contact the prospective client. Sometimes it was a phone call to talk about something she discovered about the account. Other times it was an interesting industry story she came across or a product special. After 90 days and nine contacts, the prospects would be retired to generic marketing, although she would never completely lose touch with these firms. Whenever she runs across something she thinks would be of interest to a specific prospect, she plans to keep in touch despite their not having shown any interest in her offering yet.

When I last talked to Terry, her firm had already landed a few new corporate clients and they were engaged in serious discussions with a few others. She'd also shared her strategy with several other business colleagues from different industries who were realizing very positive results as well.

Gear Up for Your Own Campaign

By conducting a professional account entry campaign focused on the customer's issues, needs, and challenges—rather than your offering—you will penetrate the decision maker's consciousness.

This is how you get name recognition. It's how you turn your company and you from an unknown entity into something familiar. It's about building relationships over time and not just about a quick sale.

As you've seen, an account entry campaign is not a passive process. It takes a lot of work and focus to make it happen; you have to keep at it for several months. But it's how you get on somebody's radar screen—which you aren't today.

When you ultimately connect, your professionalism and persistence will stand out in their minds. You have a good chance of getting at least 30 minutes of the decision maker's time. And that's how you get your foot in the door.

KEY POINTS

- Don't make one call and wait for the decision maker to phone you back. In today's business environment, that callback just doesn't happen.
- To break through the marketing clutter and get noticed by decision makers, a well-planned account entry campaign is essential.
- Well-crafted account entry campaigns share the value of working with your firm and demonstrate your firm's expertise over multiple contacts.
- Critical must-have items in your account entry tool kit include voice mail scripts, telephone scripts for speaking with a decision maker, guidelines on handling obstacles, and sample letters.
- Plan on seven to ten contacts to develop name recognition, capture your prospect's attention, and, ultimately, get your foot in the door.

12

CREATE ENTICING VOICE MAIL MESSAGES

Voice mail is a fact of life today. Whether you like it or not is irrelevant. If your livelihood depends on getting into big companies, it's imperative to learn how to use it to your advantage. What most sellers don't realize is that voice mail is an incredible tool. Because most decision makers let unrecognized callers roll into voice mail, you have an opportunity to leave a message just for them.

But will they listen? The answer is: it's entirely up to you. If you craft a tight personalized message targeted right to their needs, they will. A good voice mail differentiates you from all the other sellers vying for time on their calendar. Decision makers might not call you back right away or even at all, but you'll register with them. If you keep on implementing your account entry campaign, you'll ultimately get in.

It amazes me how many people still tell you to never, ever leave a voice mail message. They say, "Call in the early morning or after everyone leaves. That's when decision makers answer their own phones." That may be true, but if you've already left an enticing message, those same decision makers will be much more receptive to talking with you.

TOSS OUT THE TRITE AND TRADITIONAL

If you're like most sellers, when you leave a voice mail, it probably follows the following format:

Introduction	Hello, Mr./Ms. Prospect. This is (your name) calling. I'm a (your position) with (your company).
Company Overview	We make/do (fill in the blank). Our product/service is (self-serving adjectives) and (self-promoting puffery).
Reason for Call	I'd love to set up a time to find out a bit more about your needs in this area and tell you more about our new offerings.
Gracious Close	Please call me at your earliest convenience to set up a time to get together. I look forward to meeting with you. My number is . . .

What's wrong with the message? Despite the caller's intent to be courteous and informative, it sounds like a salesperson, plain and simple. Every single day decision makers hear this same message, usually with only minor variations, from a multitude of vendors.

You may have learned once that this was the proper way to leave voice mails. But the world has changed and today decision makers delete messages such as this within seconds. They aren't interested in a pitch about your company, product, or service. They're only interested in how you can make a difference in their business. That's why these tired, trite telephone scripts need to be retired.

WHAT'S ENTICING TO CORPORATE DECISION MAKERS?

Being *enticing* is about arousing the curiosity of prospective decision makers; it's about saying something that piques their interest and makes them want to learn more.

To come up with an enticing voice mail, you need to put a good amount of thought into it. There's no way around it. Provocative, alluring, and brilliant statements don't just naturally flow out of your mouth when it's time to leave a message.

You have to think like a decision maker too. What are they interested in learning more about? Here are some ideas to stimulate your thinking.

Business Results

Corporate decision makers are under extreme pressure to reach ever-increasing goals with ever-shrinking time frames and resources. They're always willing to meet with someone who can help them address their critical business issues and attain their objectives. You'll attract their attention with:

- strong value propositions,
- business-related terminology, and
- relevant success stories.

Information

Decision makers are interested in what's happening outside their own little world. If they believe you have knowledge that's of value to them, they'll be willing to meet with you. You'll find they want to learn more about

- industry trends,
- their customers,
- the marketplace,
- other areas of their own company,
- their competitors, and
- new technology.

Ideas

With time at such a premium in most big companies, decision makers don't always have the luxury of "thinking" about how to improve their business. Instead they run from meeting to meeting, putting out whatever fires emerge along the way.

Sellers who invest their own time to study the big company's business issues immediately stand out from the pack—especially if they have ideas on how to make things better. Nothing is more tempting to future customers than a good idea.

Hopefully by now you're over the delusion that decision makers are interested in your product, service, or solution. Again, it's only a tool that helps them achieve the results they need.

But look at how valuable *you* are. They want your brain, your knowledge, and your expertise in conjunction with your offering applied to their business. Demonstrate all that in your voice mail and you'll be in the door in no time flat.

ANATOMY OF AN EFFECTIVE VOICE MAIL MESSAGE

Enticing voice mail messages require careful planning and crafting. The ones that have proven effective contain the following three key elements—all of which are essential in today's crazy business environment.

1. Establish Credibility. When you leave a voice mail, your first task is to ensure that you're taken seriously from the moment your voice is heard. To establish credibility with corporate decision makers, you can reference:

- Your Referrals: If you have a referral of any sort, this is the time to use it. You might say,

  > "Mr. Graham. Brian Johnson calling. Marcia Herman from the Leadership Development Center said to give you a call."

  > "Alex. Nancy Stevens from Synergy Software. I just spoke with Bob Cummings in your corporate research area. He said that you were the person I needed to speak to."

- Your Research: So few sellers actually invest time studying their clients before placing a call that you'll immediately set yourself apart if you mention it in your voice mail. You might say,

    > "I saw in the *Wall Street Journal* that your firm's number one business priority in the upcoming year is . . . "

    > "In reviewing your company's Web site and marketing collateral, it became apparent to me that a critical issue you're facing is . . . "

    If you're not doing precall research prior to contacting a big company, you're making a huge mistake. Dig in. Do it. What you learn makes your voice mail even more enticing.

- *Triggering Events:* Mention these to let decision makers know you're up to date on what's happening in their firm. You might say,

    > "I noticed in yesterday's *Business Journal* that your company will soon be acquiring your main competitor."

    > "In the latest issue of *Industry Events,* I saw that your firm is now moving into the medical market."

2. Pique Curiosity. After reviewing what you know about your targeted big companies, determine what would pique their interest the most.

- Communicate Your Value Proposition: Prospective customers are enticed by value propositions that address critical business issues and demonstrate significant value. To increase their effectiveness, mention that the results come from businesses like theirs—or even name-drop some prominent clients. Examples of enticing value propositions include:

    > "In working with another firm like yours, we reduced space requirements by 10 percent, saving them over $500,000 on lease payments and reducing capital equipment expenditures by over $300,000."

    > "We help shrink time-to-revenue on new product introductions—a big issue facing companies today. In fact, research into failed product launches shows that

> 75 percent of executives blame weak value propositions
> as a major factor in their poor sales results."

- Share an Insightful Idea: You have to do some preliminary work to use this approach, but it's highly seductive to your prospects. To pique curiosity with a thought-provoking idea, combine it with your knowledge of their business and your value proposition. Examples might be:

> "Over the past month, I've invested a great deal of time studying your Web site and what you're trying to accomplish with it. Based on my analysis, I have some interesting ideas regarding how you could leverage it to create additional revenue opportunities."

> "I've been following your firm closely for the past six months because of its merger with Beta Industries. After hearing about your recent round of layoffs, I have some ideas that I'd like to share with you regarding how you can reduce the risks of potential legal action."

When you leave a voice mail, don't tell your customers everything. Tell them only enough to make them eager to learn more.

- Dangle Important Information: If you have access to knowledge that big company decision makers might find useful, by all means use it. One of my clients recently used this strategy to land appointments with hard-to-reach decision makers. Essentially, their salespeople said,

> "We recently conducted a study of how your customers' needs are changing relative to decisions on group life insurance. I'd like to set up a time to review some of the key points with you. I know people in your firm will be very interested in what we've uncovered."

3. Close Confidently. Enticing voice mail messages end with strength, leaving customers feeling that they'll get immediate value if they meet with you. Here are several examples that have proven to be effective:

"We should talk. The savings I'm talking about can drop right to your bottom line. Give me a call at . . . and we'll set up a time to discuss this further on the phone."

"While I can't promise you the exact same results, I can assure you that it's worth your time. My number is . . . I'll give you a call tomorrow at 10 AM to find a date that works for both of us."

"If you'd like to find out how (well-known firm) utilized similar ideas to gain significant market share, you can reach me at . . . I look forward to getting together."

Please notice how these closures demonstrate a quiet confidence and assuredness in the value of a meeting. You may set up an appointment to get together in person or your next step might be a phone conversation. In either case, you advance the sales process to its logical next step.

PULL IT ALL TOGETHER

As you can see by now, you can't just leave your voice mail message to happenstance. If you do, you're guaranteed to sound trite and cheesy—exactly like the kind of seller everyone detests.

That means you need to write a script. There's no way around it. More than anything else, script writing is about choosing the exact words that best convey to prospective buyers why they need to meet with you. When you only have a short time to leave your message, every word counts.

Please note, I didn't say you would read a script. That's for those telemarketers who bother you at home. You're going to start with a script to ensure you get your message right. When that's done, you'll work on your delivery so you sound like a human being.

In fact, you're going to need two to three different voice mail scripts, all emphasizing a slightly different aspect of your business value. Why? Remember, you're launching a campaign to get into that big company and you need to plan at least seven contacts.

Before you write your own scripts, here's an example of one "before" and two "after" voice mails so you can see the difference.

Before: Relocation Company. Martha contacted me because she was having trouble getting her foot in the door of prospective clients. This is the message she was leaving on their voice mails:

> "Good morning, Mr. Smith. My name is Martha Johnson and I sell relocation services. We are a relocation management company that works with corporations like eBay and EMC to develop and administer customized relocation programs.
>
> "We help our clients do three things: attract and retain talent, reduce the cost of relocation, and focus on their core business principles. I'd like to set up a time to talk with you about what you're doing and share with you how we handle relocation services. My number is . . ."

Why wasn't Martha's message working? The decision maker's guard immediately goes up when he learns that a sales representative is on the line. Then Martha's "pitch" further seals her fate.

While she tries to sound credible by throwing in client names and a slew of value-based buzzwords, it was a mouthful to say. She never gives any good solid reason for the decision maker to speak with her either. Finally, she ends with the trite closing comments about wanting to get together to explore his needs and share . . . blah, blah, blah.

After #1. After talking with Martha, we identified several value propositions that could be enticing to prospective customers. Plus we changed the wording to make her sound like a peer who brought value.

> "Bob. Martha Johnson from Absolute Relocation Services. I've been researching your company and the number of executive moves you handle annually. I have some ideas on how you can save significant dollars in your relocation program.
>
> "One of my recent clients (a high-tech firm like yours) just saved $⅓ million and another one saved $150,000 all because we found big errors in how their service providers were doing things. With today's tight budgets, this is money you don't need to throw away. We should talk. Again, this is Martha Johnson at . . ."

Notice how different this message sounds. Martha gets right down to business. She conveys an impression of being knowledgeable and competent. She communicates a strong value proposition and then closes with confidence.

After #2. Because you're going to have to call back, you might as well plan your second and third message from the get-go. Here is an example of the follow-up call we developed:

> "Bob. Martha Johnson from Absolute Relocation again. As I said in my previous message, I've been researching your firm and have some ideas on how you can significantly reduce relocation costs without impacting services.
>
> "Right now I'm helping one client save $½ million annually at the same time they're getting more services—and they only relocate 40 people per year. That's money you're spending that can drop right to the bottom line. Let's set up a time to talk. Again, this is Martha at . . . "

Would these messages work? Absolutely. Martha talks about a subject her decision makers want to learn more about. She demonstrates that she's invested time in their business prior to calling. She focuses on business results and shares that she has an idea for the company. She gets right to the point and doesn't waste one word.

If getting into big companies is important to you, then invest time creating a series of voice mail scripts that work. You'll find that Tool 7: Voice Mail Script Template in Appendix A will help you craft effective ones.

KEY POINTS

- While most sellers balk at scripts, they're absolutely necessary to ensure delivery of the right message and to prevent you from sounding like a blathering idiot.
- Voice mails that focus on business results are highly enticing to corporate decision makers who are faced with ever-increasing goals, limited resources, and short timeframes.

- You can establish your credibility immediately in a voice mail message by referencing your referrals, the research you've conducted, or a *triggering event.*
- Pique the decision maker's curiosity by communicating your value proposition, sharing an insightful idea, or tantalizing them with information they'd love to learn more about.
- Multiple voice mail scripts are necessary—each emphasizing a slightly different aspect of your value proposition or an idea for the decision maker's business.

13

GET READY FOR
PRIME TIME

Figuring out how to be enticing is hard work. When I first started using the new voice mail message format, it took me a while to get the hang of it. I'm not sure what was harder—keeping the message under 30 seconds or figuring out how I could effectively pique somebody's interest.

I'm embarrassed to admit that my first messages were almost 60 seconds long. I loved every single word in them. My natural instinct was to tell prospective customers as much as I could possibly squeeze into that little time frame. Rather than cut words, I tried to speak faster so I could get it all in. When it finally dawned on me that I needed a variety of follow-up messages, I realized I didn't have to cram everything into one voice mail. What a relief!

FINE-TUNE YOUR VOICE MAIL MESSAGE

Before you pick up the phone to contact a decision maker, it's a good idea to fine-tune your message. Here are several strategies I learned that really improve how you sound to potential customers.

Eliminate Self-Serving Verbiage

While you might love sharing wonderful words that describe your company, products, or services, they make you sound like a pushy salesperson. To avoid using this self-promoting puffery, remember to do the following with your voice mails:

- Cross out all adjectives and adverbs. Prospective buyers think you use words like "robust," "one-stop," and "leading edge" only because you're trying to "sell" them something. By leaving words such as these in, your credibility actually decreases.
- Omit those cute slogans describing your company. Customers could care less if you're known as the "Guardians of the Night" or if your tag line is "Quantum Leaps to Extraordinary Results." They're a complete waste of words.

Read Your Script Aloud

After writing your voice mail script, read it out loud. You'll be amazed at how differently it sounds when spoken. While your grammar teacher might be impressed with your eloquence, it doesn't work if you're trying to leave enticing messages. Make sure you:

- Use contractions. It's how people talk naturally. If you say "are not" or "let us," you sound stilted. Your goal is to sound normal, not scripted.
- Replace pretentious words. Only use words that you'd say in everyday conversation. For example, use (not utilize) "talk" instead of "dialogue" and "help" instead of "facilitate."
- Drop all company jargon. Forget using acronyms unless the whole world knows them.
- Get rid of any worn-out closes. Cross out phrases such as: "I'll be in your area next week and could stop by . . ." or "Can you think of a reason we shouldn't meet to talk more?"

Eliminate Subservient Language

This is critical especially if you're 30 years younger than the decision maker or feel like a peon compared to Mr. Bigwig. You must sound like you're talking to an equal. Your stature is immediately diminished if you sound eternally grateful to be granted a meeting. If it's culturally appropriate, use a person's first name. In the United States, it's common to address someone as Bill or Mary. In other parts of the world, it is considered rude.

TAKE YOUR MESSAGE TO THE NEXT LEVEL

The challenge of getting into big companies is formidable, but the payback can be huge. Preparing enticing voice mail messages requires some serious thinking, a good understanding of your business case, and the panache to pull it off as a professional.

How Does It *Hear?*

Just because you think your voice mail is ready for prime time doesn't mean it is. You need to conduct a *hearing* test. Why? Because it's not what you say that's important, it's what your customer hears.

So get on the phone, call your own number, and leave yourself the exact voice mail you're planning to use for a customer. Then call yourself back and see how you sound. The first time you hear yourself, you'll be appalled at how boring, dry, or nasal your voice sounds. Expect that.

Then call a second time and listen as your customer. Ask yourself, "How does it *hear?*" Play it again. If you'd call yourself back, you have a winner. If you wouldn't, go back to the drawing board and fix it. Figure out what to change so you don't sound like an overzealous pitchman, a boring drone, or groveling salesperson.

Revise and Review

Once I struggled for over a week with a message for the vice president of sales in an account I'd been following for quite a while. Suddenly a *triggering event* occurred that created tons of opportunity for my company. To get Mr. Bigshot's attention, I needed to create a strong link between his critical business issues and my offering.

No, I didn't work all day on it, but I was constantly turning it over in my mind trying to figure out what would be enticing. In between client meetings, I'd tweak my approach or find a new way to say what I meant. I must have called myself dozens of times and anguished over how dreadful my message sounded. But then suddenly, out of the ashes and rubble, a good script finally emerged. The difference was immediately apparent; it clicked.

Sometimes you have to try your script out on real prospects first to get a sense of what works or what doesn't. Don't worry about getting it perfect because it never is. Get it as close as you can, try it out, make more changes, and try it again. When your voice mail script is a winner, you're on your way to getting your foot in the door. Your follow-up messages almost seem to write themselves once you get the first message nailed down.

Worry about Content First and Style Second

Up to this point, we've focused on *what* to say because until the message is enticing, everything else is irrelevant. Anyone who tells you that you just need to have a positive attitude and sound enthusiastic hasn't tried to get into big companies in the past few years.

The ability to connect your firm's value proposition with the decision maker's priority business needs is the foundation you need to get in. It's also what you need to get over your own angst in calling. When you're confident that what you offer truly is valuable to a decision maker, it's not nearly so hard to make the call. It's still not easy for many people but if they know what to say, it's doable. And that's what counts.

THROW AWAY THE SCRIPT

After all this work to write an enticing voice mail message, when it finally comes time to use it, you have to get rid of it. That's right. When there's a script on your desk while you're making a call, it ends up getting read—despite all your best intentions. As a result, you sound canned.

So you have to get rid of it. But before tossing it into the wastebasket, practice delivering your message so you can talk it. Write down a couple of bullet points with just a few words to remind you of the essence of your message. Practice until you feel ready to make the call. Your goal is to sound like you're *talking to a peer,* not like a salesperson. Your natural aliveness needs to come through so the person on the other end of the line knows you're real.

The single most important feeling you want your prospects to have when they hear your voice mail message is a *quiet and solid confidence that you can make a difference in their business.*

Create Quick Rapport

When contacting a stranger on the phone, it's hard to establish a connection right away. I always recommend getting a quick read on the people you're calling before you actually leave a message or talk to them. The easiest way to do that is to listen to their voice mail message. Listen for these things:

- *Names.* Does the person call herself Kate, Katie, Kathryn, or Ms. Pronounced? Make sure you pay attention to how to say the decision maker's name too because you don't want to botch it when you call.
- *Pacing.* Matching a person's pacing is a quick way to make someone feel comfortable with you. If they speak slowly and distinctly, do the same. If they speak rapidly, pick up your pace.
- *Intensity.* Some people sound quiet; others exude energy. To increase their comfort level with you, mirror their intensity as best you can.

I'll never forget one customer of mine who was probably as unlike me as anyone could possibly be. He talked so slowly and deliberately that a conversation with him was painful for me. Literally. Whenever I talked with him, I needed to get into a near-comatose state in order not to totally bowl him over. But it worked; Don felt comfortable with me and my business with his firm grew.

Try to Sound Human

Last, but certainly not least, you have your own personality that absolutely needs to be incorporated into everything you do. You are not a drone or a clone. You're a unique human being with your own style.

While I firmly believe that you need to have a strong business message in your account entry campaign, your individuality needs to shine through as well. One of the most natural ways to become human to a prospective client is to have a sense of humor about yourself and the situation.

The best time to do this is in your follow-up calls. After a couple rounds of voice mail, you're probably getting a little frustrated. That's normal. Think about how you might respond in a humorous manner to someone who doesn't call you back after you'd tried to reach him several times.

I've had a lot of fun approaching follow-up calls this way. For example, I've said this to my prospects in a teasing manner:

> "Terry. Jill Konrath calling again—for the third time. I know most people aren't foolish enough to keep calling someone back who never picks up the phone.
>
> "But the reason I'm here once again is because—as I mentioned earlier—we help sales organizations shrink time-to-revenue on new product launches. I know that's important to your company because it's all over your annual report that just came out.
>
> "I've got some ideas that can help you out. Let's get together soon. My number is . . . "

Believe it or not, that kind of message even differentiates you from everyone else. You're not a robot reciting the company line. You're a human being, funny, and a welcome relief in an otherwise ordinary day. Sounding human breaks through their resistance and can even generate a call back. Or when you finally do reach them, they know who you are and remember your messages. I've even had people say to me, "I've been meaning to get back to you. Thanks for being so persistent."

EVALUATE YOUR VOICE MAILS

When push comes to shove, what counts in the end is that your messages resonate with your prospective buyer. Believe me, it's better to learn this now than to put all your hopes on an account entry strategy that's ineffective. Use the Customer Hearing Test on the following page to evaluate your voice mails.

Involve a Trusted Colleague

For the best results, get a colleague involved to give you an outside opinion. Prior to starting, give her an overview of your customer's business and their needs. Ask her to imagine that she's just returned to her desk after a three-hour meeting and has 20 minutes before an important conference call. When she checks her voice mail, she hears, "You have nine new messages." Yours is the seventh one in the queue. She's busy and doesn't have time to waste on self-serving salespeople.

Tell her you need feedback about how your message sounds. Ask her to be brutally honest since that's the only way you'll learn if your message breaks through all the clutter. When she's done listening, ask her to answer the questions on the next page with her initial and immediate reactions. Customers don't pontificate about your message. They make snap decisions to either listen to your message or delete it. That's what you need to know.

Take the Customer Hearing Test

Tell your colleague that if she agrees with the questions on the next page, she should make a check in the space provided. If she doesn't agree, she should leave the space blank.

When your colleague is finished answering the questions, ask her to explain her gut-level reactions as best she can. If she says you sound cheesy, accept it and figure out how to make your message sound better. If she tells you that you sound desperate, find out why and change what you say and how you say it. If she says that you sound exactly like the other 30 salespeople who called today, have her tell you what makes you sound that way. Finally, find out if she would have deleted your message

_____ 1. The caller immediately sounded (tone of voice, confidence) like a businessperson.

_____ 2. Credibility was established within ten seconds. The caller referenced (*check which method was used*)
    _____ a. research conducted prior to phoning.
    _____ b. referral from a credible colleague.
    _____ c. recent event that happened in my company.

_____ 3. The caller used business terminology and focused on business results important to my company. No mention was made of products, services, or solutions.

_____ 4. My interest was piqued and I wanted to learn more. The caller (*check which method was used*)
    _____ a. shared a strong value proposition, complete with statistics and data to support it.
    _____ b. referred to how a firm similar to mine achieved business goals or solved key challenges.
    _____ c. mentioned ideas related to helping me achieve critical business objectives.
    _____ d. referenced important information I'd love to learn more about.

_____ 5. Closed with confidence and left me feeling that she or he could make a difference for my company.

at any point prior to its ending—and, if so, why. (Check out Tool 8: The Voice Mail Evaluator in Appendix A to pinpoint additional reasons why prospects might delete your message.)

Use these assessments as a quick way to improve yourself before you make contact with an actual prospect. If your voice mail doesn't pass these tests, it's imperative to understand why. You need this tough feedback to figure out what changes need to be made. When you're trying to get into big companies, you can't be sloppy in your approach.

While these strategies don't guarantee a victory over voice mail, they do ensure that you stand out from the crowd. Creating a series of enticing messages enables you to penetrate your customer's natural defenses. When you do connect, getting an appointment is the natural next step. And, don't be too surprised if you pick up the phone one day and it's your prospective customer—begging to meet with you!

KEY POINTS

- Voice mail messages that contain self-serving verbiage or focus on your offering are deleted immediately.
- Practice your script aloud because how you talk is very different from how you write. Make sure you speak like a normal person.
- Leave your message on your own voice mail system to hear how you sound first. Revise it until you're comfortable with the key points, the flow, and your own confidence.
- Have a trusted colleague evaluate your script prior to using it on a prospective client. Use their honest feedback to make it better.
- Always ask, "How does the message *hear?*" from a customer's perspective. That's what counts.

14

PROVOCATIVE WRITTEN COMMUNICATIONS

For years I told people to not waste their time writing letters to prospective clients. Why? Because they'd agonize for weeks over what to put in it, debating each little word and all its nuances. Then they'd send out a bunch of letters to their mailing list, sit back, and wait for the phone to ring. When the first week passed with no response, they remained hopeful. But after a month with no callbacks, they were downright depressed. The worst thing was that they were no closer to landing a new customer than they were when they started.

I still feel the same way about using letters as your main account entry strategy. The phone needs to be your primary tool to get your foot in the door of big companies. But written communications such as e-mails, faxes, and handwritten notes support your phone calls and are an important part of your tool kit too.

TARGETED LETTERS FOR TARGETED PROSPECTS

Forget doing any bulk mailings if you're selling to big companies. They're utterly worthless for getting the attention of corporate decision makers. Don't waste your time (or money) sending brochures or catalogs either. Prospects will quickly glance at anything you send, mentally note that they already have a supplier, and toss it in their circular file—more commonly known as the wastebasket.

When you set your eyes on getting into a particular big company, you are doing one-on-one marketing. It's you writing to one person. That's all. Totally personalized. Totally customized.

> Every piece of correspondence sent to your targeted account must be written specifically for the decision maker with whom you want to meet.

To be irresistible to prospective customers, your writing must accomplish two things:

1. Pique their curiosity by speaking directly to their business issues and challenges.
2. Position your firm as a competent resource capable of making a difference.

These are exactly the same things you need to do with your voice mail messages. All the work you've done so far can be used in your correspondence too. No more research either. You've already done that; recreating the wheel isn't necessary.

WHAT'S WRONG WITH THIS LETTER?

Your challenge is to use the information you've uncovered to craft a letter that acts like a magnet. When prospective buyers read it, they should instantly want to know more. Yet most correspondence falls miserably short of achieving the seller's desired objective.

On the following page is an example of a typical sales letter. See if you can identify what's wrong with it as you read.

JumpStart
Product Launch Services

Dear Mr. Prospect,

Are you introducing important new products in the upcoming months? For most companies, the success of their new products is vital to the financial health of their organization. Yet in today's challenging business environment, it's never been more difficult to capture that ever-shrinking window of opportunity.

At JumpStart, we offer a wide range of services that can help your company as you launch these new products. We can help you find your value proposition, create customer-ready sales messaging, and create powerful sales tools for your salespeople to use during sales calls. Additionally we can help you train your sales force on "how to sell" the new products, and we're able to do it in a variety of mediums such as workshops, Webinars, teleseminars, or even one-on-one coaching.

Our firm is well known in St. Paul, having been in business for 17 years. We've worked with a variety of clients so have expertise in numerous areas. What makes us different from other firms is our passion for what we do, our creativity, our integrity, and our commitment to excellence in client relationships. We are passionate about being the best in these areas.

I would welcome the chance to discuss your product launch needs with you to see if some opportunities exist for us to assist you. If we can be of service to you in any way, please call me at (651) xxx-xxxx. The first hour of consultation is free and I would be delighted to hear from you.

Sincerely yours,

Chris

Chris Alstead
JumpStart Product Launch Services

Enc. Corporate Brochure

If you're like most people who read this letter, you probably think it sounds pretty good. It may even look pretty similar to your own best efforts. But it's not effective, and that's the only thing that matters. Here's an analysis.

The Opening Isn't Customized

Letters need to capture a prospect's attention right away. This one starts with a question—which can be a great way to draw people in. Unfortunately, the question isn't tailored to this particular prospect's business situation. Then the text that follows sounds like it came from a brochure or magazine article.

This opening leads the reader to believe the seller hasn't invested one iota of time understanding his business needs or concerns. He's getting pure boilerplate material—the same pabulum that's being dished out to every other prospective buyer in the world.

The Body Lacks Focus

In the second paragraph, the seller tries to impress the prospect with the wide range of services her company offers. She's also hoping that when her prospect reads it, he'll find something in the laundry list that he needs right now, thus opening the door for her. Instead of helping her accomplish her desired outcome, it actually detracts from it. Her firm looks like it lacks focus and expertise; she looks like she's groping in the dark for business.

The third paragraph is the seller's attempt to differentiate her company from other available alternatives out there. While she thinks her comments on working with a "variety of clients" enhance her position, her prospect feels very differently. He wants to work with someone who knows his business, a company he doesn't have to bring up to speed. The seller is also trying to impress the prospect with what a wonderful company she works for, but her reader writes it all off as self-serving hyperbole, thus diminishing her in his eyes.

The Close Is Weak

While trying to be gracious, the seller has just made herself sound like every other salesperson. While she would "welcome" a chance to get together and be of "service," she's given him no reason to take time from his busy schedule. She's the only one who gets value from the meeting.

Then because she doesn't want to be "pushy," the seller invites the prospect to call her. Following up is her responsibility, not his. To off-load this task to him is unprofessional—as is her offer to give away an hour of time at this point. This does *not* incentivize a corporate decision maker. Time is what's lacking in his life; the last thing he wants to do is spend it being "sold."

She closes with the statement that she'd be "delighted" to hear from him. I bet she would; it gives her an opportunity to sell. But does it make her sound like a peer? No way. She sounds like a person who would be grateful for a meager spot of his time. Finally, she throws in the brochure as a last ditch hope that he'll find something in it he likes and give her a call. Unfortunately, it's going right into the garbage can.

There, you've seen it. A beautifully crafted sales letter torn to shreds. After all the effort was put into creating this "masterpiece," you'd certainly hope for better feedback and stellar results.

Unfortunately, the seller has fallen into exactly the same trap that leads to such lousy voice mails. Instead of focusing on her customer, it's all about me, me, me. In her letter, she never mentioned what she knew about the client—even though she may have invested hours learning about his business. Her value proposition has disappeared, and she's clearly forgotten the language of business.

WHAT MAKES THIS LETTER
WORTH READING?

To write an *effective* letter for your account entry campaign, forget all that old garbage that clutters your mind about good sales letters. Everything you learned is passé and doesn't work anymore. Creating an effective letter is very similar to crafting your voice mail script. They build on each other and integrate the same message.

JumpStart
Product Launch Services

Dear Mr. Prospect,

With your company's recent spin-off from Galaxy, Inc., the success of your new product line is imperative. Miss your forecast and Wall Street will be all over you. There's no room for error.

We work with technology-driven firms like yours to shrink time-to-revenue on new product introductions. Specifically, we help our clients:

- **Reduce ramp-up time.** We get your salespeople out there with customers, doing the right things to drive sales immediately. A recent client exceeded their revenue goals by 27 percent in the first month, 19 percent in the second month, and 32 percent in the third month after launch.

- **Minimize nonselling activities.** We significantly cut the 40 to 60 hours per month the average salesperson spends creating customized materials for your customers. We keep them out selling, where they belong!

- **Increase their sales velocity.** More than anything, we shrink your sales cycle. When customers feel there are valid business reasons for spending money, they part with it much sooner. Many of our clients cut several months out of their typical 9-month to 12-month sales cycles.

As I said in my phone message last week, we can make a big difference for your company as you move ahead with your product launches. Let's get together to discuss this in more depth. I know you'll be interested in learning how we've helped other firms achieve significant results.

I'll call you next Tuesday at 7:45 AM to set up a time when we can get together.

Sincerely yours,

Chris

Chris Alstead
JumpStart Product Launch Services

Take a look at another letter from the exact same seller on the previous page. Her offering is identical, but how she talks about it is fundamentally different.

If you were the vice president of sales, which letter would attract your attention? Same company, same offering. But if you received the first letter, you wouldn't have a clue what difference the seller's firm could make for your business. Let's take a closer look at what makes the second letter so strong and effective.

The Opening Hooks the Reader

From the very first sentence, it's clear the seller knows what's happening in the decision maker's world. The company has spun off from its parent firm and Wall Street is watching. Also, the seller is well aware that new products are vital to the success of this firm. The decision maker is hooked right away.

The Body Highlights Outcomes

Immediately the seller positions her firm as an expert in helping similar companies achieve a critical business result that is important to the decision maker.

Then, in quick succession are three bullets highlighting the specific outcomes this firm can help their clients achieve (their value proposition). To ensure the key points can quickly be assimilated, the short statements netting out the impact are also bolded. To make these points even stronger, relevant statistics are included. Everything is about the results and outcomes of working with the firm. Business terminology is used throughout.

The seller's credibility comes from focusing on this, rather than trying to prove it by using a bunch of overused adjectives or puffed up, inflated verbiage about the firm.

The Close Promises Value

To wrap up this letter, the seller summarizes the value she can bring. Then she suggests getting together in a manner that makes it clear she is bringing something worthwhile to the meeting. She's not a hopeful seller, grateful for a chance to meet the almighty corporate buyer. She brings value herself.

Her last sentence clarifies exactly when she will follow up to set up this meeting. It's short and to the point, increasing the likelihood that her prospect will take her call. Also, it's easier to catch prospects prior to meetings in the morning, before or after the lunch hour, very late in the afternoon, or even after hours.

This last letter works. Decision makers in big companies would pay attention to it. Guaranteed. They still might not pick up the phone to call you back, and it's still hard to catch them at their desk. But you're on their radar screen now. Follow up with another phone call or send over a relevant article. It's just a matter of time before you connect and get your initial meeting set up. And remember, the appointment may be in person or over the phone; it doesn't matter—just so long as it advances the sales process.

HOW TO WRITE CUSTOMER-ATTRACTING LETTERS

As a baseline, let me say, "No Typos." I'd like to believe that's self-evident, but experience tells me otherwise. Spell check and grammar check every single letter that goes out with your name on it. Have someone else read it too. It's awfully embarrassing if you have "manger" instead of "manager" or "asses" instead of "assets." Plus, make sure you spell everyone's name right.

In case you're wondering if you should use first names or not, there's no hard and fast rule. In the United States, using someone's first name is commonplace and very acceptable. However, if you're not comfortable using first names, don't. In other countries, it's often totally unacceptable to use proper names in addressing someone you don't know—even in a letter. Check with your peers or colleagues to make your decision. Go with the cultural norms.

Here's what you need to remember when you write letters as part of your account entry campaign.

Do

To capture the attention of the decision maker in your targeted account, make sure that you:

- Do demonstrate your knowledge of their company. Mention the *triggering event* that caused you to take notice of what's happening in their company. Show you've done your homework.
- Do speak the language of business. Remember, customers could care less about your product or service. It's only a tool that enables them to achieve their objectives or solve problems.
- Do share your value proposition. Highlight any key metrics that demonstrate the outcomes of working with your firm. Use industry statistics to support your position.
- Do write as if you're communicating to a peer. If you sound like you're groveling, no one will want to meet with you—no matter what position they hold in the company.
- Do make it easy to scan. Your reader should easily be able to pick out the main points. Use bullets; three is best. And make sure the text immediately following the bullets is in bold.
- Do share customer results. Build credibility by highlighting business results achieved by similar customers. Be as specific as you can.

Don't

Make sure you avoid these problem areas when you write your customer-enticing letters:

- Don't talk about your product or service. They're essentially irrelevant. Remember, they're just tools.
- Don't brag about your company. Anything you do to differentiate your firm sounds cheesy when they haven't decided to change yet.
- Don't use pleasantries or small talk. Decision makers don't want to be introduced to your company. They don't care if you're the new person in town.
- Don't use subservient language. Words such as "delighted," "pleased," and "honored" make you sound like a lightweight.

Following these guidelines will have a huge impact on the effectiveness of your correspondence. Don't be concerned that you aren't pointing out how wonderful your organization is. The strength and capability of your company shines through the letter. It is so far above what decision makers see every day that you'll stand high above the crowd.

KEY POINTS

- The most common mistake in crafting a letter is to focus on how great your firm or offering is. These mailings are immediately tossed into the wastebasket.
- Total personalization is essential for penetrating big accounts. Write your letter specifically for the decision maker you want to meet.
- Always write as if you're communicating to a peer. Subservient language positions you as a lightweight not worth meeting.
- Catch a decision maker's attention right away with a comment demonstrating up-to-date knowledge of their company or by referencing a strong referral.
- To create a customer-enticing letter, make sure the business value of working with your firm is highlighted with bullet points and bold type. Be very explicit in terms of outcomes.

15

LEVERAGE E-MAIL
STRATEGIES TO GET IN

Leveraging e-mail as an account entry strategy will never replace the phone, but it may be more effective for reaching certain people. Some decision makers spend hours each day online sorting through and responding to e-mail. Others travel so often that e-mail may be the only way you'll ever catch them. Done well, e-mails can be a valuable addition to your account entry tool kit.

The first time I used e-mail to get my foot in the door I wasn't sold on its effectiveness. I'm not sure what surprised me most—that I got a response at all or that it came in less than a day. When corporate decision makers check their e-mail, they typically take extremely quick action on their messages so that their inbox doesn't get filled up.

When you use e-mail to connect with a prospective customer, you need to approach it with as much forethought as all your other account entry strategies. Just because it's so easy to dash off a message doesn't mean you should. In fact, just the opposite is true. When "go" or "no go" decisions are made from just a few paragraphs, your word choices are even more important.

Perhaps the most critical thing to remember about using e-mail is people's high sensitivity to spam. Unless you've crafted a very well-written message, you could easily be considered a "spammer," and that is the kiss of death to your sales efforts.

How do you get people's e-mail addresses? The simplest way is ask for them. When someone in the big company tells you that Sandy Wallace is the decision maker, mention that you'd like Sandy's e-mail address too so you can send some information. If you sound professional and ask confidently, it's highly likely that you'll get it.

AVOID WRITING MESSAGES
THAT GET DELETED

Because e-mails are typically pretty short, it's a real challenge to determine what to put in your message to a corporate decision maker.

Just the other day I got an e-mail with a subject line that read, "XZY Research." In the "from" line was an AOL address. Not a good sign to start with, and things went downhill fast from there. With a few minor alterations to protect the misguided salesperson from embarrassment, see the next page for what it said.

What's wrong with this e-mail? First, it immediately starts out with the "all about me" content that so many sellers feel compelled to use. He clearly doesn't know anything about my company because his expertise doesn't align with my business-to-business niche. As a reader, I was turned off right away.

Second, the hapless seller proceeded to share every possible thing his company did, hoping that something would stick. Instead, his firm looks desperate: "Here's our laundry list. Perhaps you'll need something on it!"

Third, I was stunned when he proposed a business relationship. My only thoughts were, "Why in the world would I bring an absolute stranger in to work with my customers?" He's asking me to risk my best resource for a few bucks. Clearly he doesn't understand the value of a strong client relationship and how easily it can be damaged.

Finally, he sent along an attachment for my further reading pleasure. My fear of getting a computer virus kept me from opening it. But, based on what he said in the e-mail, I'm sure it was all about his company. As you can imagine, this e-mail was immediately deleted.

Dear Jill,

I would like to introduce myself and Generic Research to you. We are a full-service, global-marketing research firm based in Memphis, Tennessee, with offices in Boston and London.

We specialize in qualitative and quantitative marketing research and consulting for consumer and health-care industries.

Our services include the following:

- Focus groups
- Surveys
- Brand identity packages
- Brand development research
- Market share studies
- Marketing planning
- (13 more were actually listed)

We offer over 25 years of specialized health-care expertise and have completed projects in all industries.

I would like to discuss the opportunity of developing a business relationship with your company. For every solid referral you send our way that turns into a contract, we will pay you 15 percent commission. More information about our firm is included in the PDF files attached to this e-mail.

Please feel free to contact me directly to discuss this in further detail. Thank you for your time and consideration. I look forward to hearing from you.

Sincerely,
Jose Montinerro

Signature [SIG] file with title and full contact information

HOW TO WRITE GREAT E-MAILS

E-mails call for a different style of writing than letters do. In some ways, it's a more casual medium although sloppiness of any sort is unacceptable. Every message you send needs to be:

- *Personalized.* Decision makers must know beyond a shadow of a doubt that you wrote this message just for them. That means you need to reference something very specific about their business.
- *Tied to their business needs.* The focus can't be on your company, product, service, or solution. It has to be related to their issues, concerns, problems, and challenges.
- *Short and pithy.* In less than 20 seconds, people decide if they'll zap e-mails, read further, or forward it to someone else. It's critical to get right to the point.
- *A conversation starter.* Good e-mails engage the reader in an online discussion. You might ask a question, invite the reader to an event, or see if they're interested in learning more about a topic.
- *Readable from a preview window.* Many people just do a quick scan of the message from their preview screen. Good e-mails get their message across quickly.

In addition, it's critical to avoid any words that might be found in a typical spammer's message. Words such as these are not only red flags for spam filters, but they announce you as a vendor: *free, secret, truth, enlarge, click here, spam, low prices, affordable, special offer, instant, massive.*

Use short paragraphs with no more than two to three sentences in them. Your grammar teacher may have told you that each paragraph should contain a fully developed thought, but she probably didn't write for online reading, which requires a different approach. To enhance readability, put a space between paragraphs. Also consider using bullet points if you're including three or more points in one sentence.

Make sure to use a screen-friendly font such as Verdana, Arial, or Helvetica. While highly stylized fonts and the use of color in your text or background may look wonderful to you, many corporate decision makers view them as quite amateurish. Using capital letters in your e-mails is the online equivalent of shouting and is considered extremely rude behavior.

Even if you have the capability to send a fancy looking html message, don't. They're much more likely to be caught in the spam filters. Worse yet, decision makers perceive them as e-brochures foisted upon them by self-serving salespeople. Unless you're a really talented graphics person, they often look tacky to someone who works for a large corporation.

Finally, don't try to save time by sending the same e-mail to a bunch of companies at the same time. It just doesn't work from a sales effectiveness standpoint. Bland boilerplate text never entices customers to take action.

CREATE MESSAGES THAT ELICIT RESPONSES

Fortunately, outside of style considerations, good e-mail messages are nearly identical to well-written letters and voice-mail messages. They follow this now-familiar three-part format:

1. *Establish credibility.* Do this by:
   - referencing a referral,
   - noting the research you've conducted, and
   - mentioning a *triggering event.*
2. *Pique curiosity.* You can make this happen by:
   - communicating your value proposition,
   - citing results your customers have realized,
   - asking a question, and
   - conveying an idea relevant to their business needs.
3. *Close graciously.* Do this by inviting a nonthreatening response.

To give you a better feel for how this works, let me share a bit more about my very first experience with cold e-mailing. Several years ago, a prestigious local radio station announced the purchase of a small station. Their intent? To provide business programming all day long.

This got me thinking about doing my own radio show. But before long the idea morphed into a "Board of Directors" program featuring different experts each day of the week. After playing with the concept for a while, I was ready to talk about it with the station's general manager. I crafted the following e-mail message to send to him:

Bob,

Congratulations on the new radio station. It's a great concept and much needed here in the Twin Cities.

For the past couple of weeks, I've invested considerable time reviewing your programming. Based on what I see, it appears your target demographic is small-sized to medium-sized businesses.

I have an idea for a show that fills a gap in your programming and would be of high interest to the management teams of these companies.

If you'd like to learn more, let me know. We can set up a time to get together.

Regards,
Jill Konrath

Signature [SIG] file with title and full contact information

This 90-word e-mail elicited a response in less than 24 hours. His e-mail back to me was terse, but it opened the door. It simply said: "Talk to Wendy, my program director." Bob copied her on this e-mail as well. Within a week, I was sitting in her office discussing the concept. For a variety of reasons, my show concept never turned into reality, but I did get my foot in the door.

Why did my e-mail work? The opening showed I was up to date on what was happening at his company. The second paragraph demonstrated that I had done my homework. The third paragraph piqued his interest with an idea. And the final paragraph was a simple call to action—did he want to learn more?

On the next page is another example of an e-mail message that works. This e-mail captures the reader's attention with a referral and then immediately focuses on the issues facing the prospective customer. Credibility is enhanced by the reference to the company's press release and connecting it to relevant business outcomes.

At the end, the seller closes by graciously giving the reader a simple choice of "yes" or "no." It's a simple, nonmanipulative way to interact with

John,

Cory Stanton suggested that I get in touch with you regarding waste reduction in your firm.

I noticed in the recent second-quarter press release that your CEO said improving operational efficiency was critical this year. In working with our clients, we typically reduce waste by a minimum of I percent to 2 percent.

I'm not sure of the status of your firm's waste reduction initiatives, but if this is of interest, let's set up a time to talk.

Sincerely,
Lane

SIG file

P.S. If you're not the one responsible for this, could you please let me know who I should be contacting?

corporate decision makers. By being nonmanipulative, if you find yourself talking to the wrong person, it's easy to get referred to the right one.

What's most important to remember is that you are not selling your products, services, or solutions. Don't mention them in your correspondence with potential clients. Focus only on their business, their issues, and their needs.

Be careful. Old habits die hard, and, if you're like most people, you love to tell about your product, service, or solution. Before you know it, you're doing it again in an e-mail. Stop, stop, stop! Selling is not about telling the world how wonderful your offering is. It's about helping customers achieve their business objectives. Always keep your focus there.

SELECT ENTICING SUBJECT LINES

Effective e-mails start out with an enticing subject line. When your prospective customers scan the contents of their inbox, you want your message to jump out at them and to say, "Read me!"

Many sellers think it's a good idea to put their company name or product offering on the subject line. Nothing could be further from the truth. Decision makers from big companies don't have extra time in their schedule to read what appears to be a sales pitch. These types of e-mails are deleted unopened.

So what entices them to look at your e-mail? A referral works extremely well if you're fortunate enough to have one. If the decision maker has no idea who you are, mention the person who referred you in the subject line. If you've read about an important *triggering event,* make note of that in your subject line. Reference an idea you have or the business results your customers realize. State that you need help or have a question.

Here are a variety of subject lines that you could adapt for your own e-mail account entry campaigns.

Subject: Mary Jones suggested I give you a call
Subject: Quick question re: waste reduction initiative
Subject: Operational efficiency problems in plant
Subject: CEO's office recommended I talk with you
Subject: Local tax incentives help firm's expansion
Subject: Need help re: document management issues
Subject: Shrinking time-to-market on new product launch
Subject: Referred to you by Bob Smith in regional office
Subject: Impact of new legislation on your HR group
Subject: Increasing sales of Star seafood products
Subject: Programming idea for new radio station
Subject: How Goodies Restaurants cut absenteeism 34 percent

Please notice, with the exception of the referrals, the above subject lines are all about what the customer is interested in, not about your offering. Additionally, only the first word is capitalized unless proper names are mentioned. Capping everything makes it look like a sales pitch.

The use of e-mail as an account entry strategy is expected to grow rapidly in the upcoming years. Learning how to leverage e-mail strategies before everyone jumps on the bandwagon gives you an advantage.

Personalization is critical. It shows corporate decision makers that you've sought them out specifically and have information that can help them eliminate problems or achieve their objectives.

Keep your e-mails conversational and short. In your initial contact, 100 to 150 words are more than enough. Ensure that each e-mail ends with something the decision maker can do, if interested, to advance the process.

Finally, make sure all your contact information is included in your signature (SIG) file. At minimum, this includes your full name, phone number, and e-mail address. Otherwise, you may be seen as a slippery character, and that's not conducive to your sales efforts.

KEY POINTS

- E-mail communication is rapidly emerging as another vehicle for capturing the attention of corporate decision makers.
- Just because it's so easy to write an e-mail doesn't mean you should send it off without a lot of forethought. Craft your e-mails as carefully as your letters.
- In your e-mails, immediately reference a referral, a *triggering event,* or something very specific regarding the prospect's business. This reference is essential so the decision maker knows it's not spam.
- E-mail writing requires a different style. Get right to the point. In just 20 seconds your prospects decide if it's worthwhile reading, if they should respond, or if they should forward it to someone else.
- The subject line is crucial in determining if your e-mail is opened. Spend time crafting a solid yet enticing subject line that begs to be read.

Part Four

BREAK THROUGH
THE BARRIERS

16

BECOME IRRESISTIBLE TO DECISION MAKERS

Believe it or not, sometimes you actually end up speaking to a real live person when you call. After experiencing what seems like an eternity of voice mail purgatory, this can be a real shock to your system.

When I restarted my business after it crashed, I identified companies I wanted to work with, conducted due diligence on them, and developed a series of magnetic messages designed to get me an appointment with those corporate decision makers. But despite my preparation, I still put off making the calls for as long as I could. It is always hard to contact strangers—even for me!

Finally, I couldn't avoid it any longer. Taking a look at my Top Ten list, my eyes zeroed in on the number one prospect. I reviewed my perfectly crafted script, took a deep breath, and dialed.

The phone rang. I stood up—erect, with good posture to ensure the best possible voice quality. It rang again. I smiled to ensure I sounded approachable—personable. It rang again.

"This is Peter," the voice said in a brisk British accent. I waited for the voice mail to continue, ready to deliver my message at the sound of the beep. There was a pause—a long, silent pause.

Suddenly I realized I was actually speaking to the vice president of sales and marketing. These bigwigs never answer their phones in the middle of the day. My mind went totally blank. Everything I had planned to say disappeared. Words came pouring out of my mouth. I bumbled. I stumbled. I sounded about as stupid as anyone could possibly sound.

Sure enough, the VP quickly cut in and put me out of my misery. "We handle all that internally," he said.

Normally I'd take that comment in stride and neutralize it without missing a beat. Instead all I wanted to do was to get off the phone—as soon as humanly possible.

"Thank you for your time," I said quickly and hung up. Shaking my head at my own incredible stupidity, I started to laugh and laugh. Things couldn't have gone worse, that's for sure. But I did learn an invaluable lesson. As a seller, you have to be ready to talk to a real person every single time you make a phone call.

Connecting with a real decision maker can easily be perceived as a "do or die" situation. Fortunately, it's not. They forget about you even before they've hung up. You can try again in another month.

GET GROUNDED BEFORE YOU CALL

But trying again later is not the point. You want to get in now! That's why you've done your research, created enticing voice mail messages, and developed provocative written communications. All the hard work you've done to this point will serve you well when you actually get a person on the line.

You're probably worried, though, about what you can say to *convince* a corporate decision maker to meet with you. Right? Let me make this perfectly clear: If you focus on touting your company, products, services, awards, or uniqueness, nothing you say will work. That's *pitching,* and decision makers hate it.

They also despise any tricky, slimy manipulative tricks of the trade that many salespeople have used for decades. So relax. You don't have to use any of the icky stuff you detest so much. The moment people feel like they're being manipulated, their defense mechanisms go up and they move into a protective mode.

Your entire approach needs to be pressure-free and focused on making a difference. You have a valid business reason for calling that can have a positive impact on their operations. Keep that in mind at all times. When you realize this from deep down inside, you don't feel like a smarmy seller or an unwanted pest.

What you do is extremely valuable. If you aren't sure of this yet, go back and refocus on understanding your firm's value proposition. When you know the difference you make, you know you've earned the right to talk to corporate decision makers.

PRACTICAL TACTICAL IDEAS

Before you pick up the phone to start calling, study the techniques discussed below. I strongly recommend you consider using them.

Set Up an Enabling Environment

Prior to making any calls, set up your environment. Clear your desk so you're not distracted with anything else. Have your voice mail bullet points close at hand as well as your plan for what you'll talk about should someone answer. You need their guidance to ensure that you cover the key points and ask the right questions.

Make sure you have paper and a pen handy too. When you get someone on the phone, take copious notes of everything that's said. Taking notes is essential. Your brain cannot possibly remember all the information that's shared with you.

Bunch Your Calls

Making one call here and another call there is a set-up for failure. Block out a couple hours at a time to make these phone calls. This allows you to get on a roll. Because it's so hard to get started calling, once you're at it you might as well keep going. Plus you become more conversational and less robotic when you get in the flow.

Make Low-Priority Calls First

Calling on your less important prospects is probably the opposite of everything you've been taught. But there is a method to this madness. When you start, you're not at your best. It takes a while to get warmed up. You may initially get thrown for a loop by the questions or comments that decision makers throw at you. Don't start calling your most desired customers first when your likelihood of blowing it is the highest. Always begin with your lower priority prospects.

Clarify Your Objective

If you do reach someone on the phone, what would you like to happen next? It's important to know before you begin, because you'll want to suggest the logical next step at the end of your conversation. You may want to arrange a follow-up phone call with the decision maker, schedule a meeting with him or her or get someone signed up for a Webinar. Just know what you want before you begin.

Identify Key Words to Listen For

When you're talking to a decision maker, listen for certain words that indicate that there may be an opportunity for your offering. When I hear these words, my ears always perk up:

- Difficulties, problems, concerns, issues
- Bottlenecks, challenges, frustrations
- Doing okay, reasonably satisfied, not thrilled

Why? Because, despite the fact that decision makers may downplay the severity of their concerns, it indicates that potential exists to get your foot in the door. Every time you hear one of these words, you need to learn more about what's happening. Asking questions is the only way to get the information you need.

Additionally, you want to listen for business trends that may not be going in the most desirable direction. For example, stagnant sales or the late introduction of a new product are things that drive my customers crazy. Look back at your enabling conditions (Chapter 5) to identify those factors that you need to be listening for when you talk to corporate decision makers.

CREATE CONVERSATIONS, DON'T MAKE PITCHES

Think calm, cool, and collected. That's how you want your presence to feel on the other end of the line. You want these potential buyers to feel that you:

- have a depth of knowledge regarding their business,
- understand the business challenges they're facing and have dealt with them before, and
- have insights, ideas, or information that would be valuable to them.

They will never, ever, in a million years feel that way if you launch into a pitch about your products or services. What you want to create is a conversation with decision makers that doesn't put them on the defensive.

Get Started

The last thing you want to do is to talk with someone who's distracted. Trying to engage people in a discussion when their mind is elsewhere is totally pointless and inane. It's also very self-absorbed thinking. Treat the person you contact like a human being, not a prospect. If you were calling a colleague, you would:

- automatically ask if you were interrupting: "Tony. Faith Walston here. Is this a good time to talk?"
- notice if they sounded distracted and address it head on: "If you're swamped right now, I don't want to interrupt. I'd rather catch you when you have a few minutes to talk."
- immediately suggest a future contact, initiated by you: "When is a good time to call you back?"

There are also phrases you need to avoid when you're calling a corporate decision maker. These comments get you in trouble nearly every time. Make sure you *never* say:

- "Thank you so much for taking my call. I really appreciate it." This statement makes you sound like you're a little person not worthy of this attention. It's not how a peer talks.
- "I'll be brief. I know how busy you are." This remark makes you sound like what you have to talk about isn't very important. You may think it sounds respectful, but instead it diminishes you.
- "How are you today?" Avoid using this question and other artificial niceties to get a conversation started. You hate it when telemarketers use these insincere and feeble attempts to warm you up. Don't make the same mistake.
- "Can you help me out?" Don't ask this question when you're talking to a person whom you know is a decision maker. This query is fine when you're searching for one, but totally inappropriate when you're talking to one. Why? Because the next thing you'll do is ask who makes decisions in this area, which immediately positions you as a seller!

THE BUSINESS-TO-BUSINESS CONVERSATION

If the decision makers say they have a few minutes or that now is as good a time as any, you've been given permission to begin your discussion. Do not launch into a spiel about your product or service or you'll blow it. I know I've told you this before, but until I'm sure it's sunk in I'll keep repeating it.

Selling is about helping your customers achieve their goals and objectives. It's about helping them get rid of their problems. It's not about what you sell. So keep your focus where it belongs—on your customer. That's what your phone conversation needs to be about.

Think about structuring your conversation just like you did in your voice-mail messages. Basically you need to do these three things:

1. Establish credibility. This helps your customers understand that you're worth listening to. It shows them that you've done your homework or have worked with similar firms. They need to feel comfortable that you're a credible resource. If you have a referral, use it now. If not, you can:

- mention the research and analysis you did prior to initiating contact;
- reference the *triggering event* that you noticed, read about, and researched; or
- cite the work you've done with similar businesses in related market segments.

2. Pique curiosity. To get prospective customers to engage in a dialogue, you need to arouse their interest. They only care about things that relate directly to their business needs—not your product or service. Again, you're not trying to sell. You're trying to establish that talking with you is worth their time.

Stimulating curiosity on the phone requires using messages nearly identical to those you developed for your voice-mail message. To capture their attention, you'll want to:

- communicate the business results that your customers have realized;
- bring up the critical issues and challenges that similar customers are facing relevant to your offering;
- share your thoughts on key problem areas related to a *triggering event;* or
- convey the essence of the important information you possess and how it could help their business.

It's imperative that whatever you say be delivered in a quiet, confident manner—very businesslike. If you sound even the least bit "rah-rah," there's a good chance you'll create immediate resistance. Never once do you mention your product, service, or solution.

3. Engage in dialogue. This is the first chance you have to actively engage your prospect in a discussion. You get to find out how interested the decision maker is in solving the problems you address, the gaps you help them close, or the goals you can help them achieve.

How do you do this? Ask questions. It's as simple as that. The best questions are provocative. They elicit the decision maker's opinion or perspective on an issue relevant to the business problem or challenge.

After you pique the decision maker's interest, continue with a question similar to these:

- Is this a concern of your firm?
- How satisfied are you with the performance of . . . ?
- Are you experiencing similar challenges?
- How concerned are you about your group's ability to . . . ?
- Is this something you're interested in learning more about?
- What is your organization doing to address these issues?
- How are you handling the . . . related to the *triggering event?*
- Do you feel you're at risk in this area?
- Have you analyzed the impact on your organization?
- What plans do you have in place to help you achieve those stretch goals?

Don't ask tricky or manipulative questions. People hate it when salespeople say, "If I could show you a way to reduce your costs by 50 percent, would you be interested?" Those questions are set-ups, and everyone knows it. They make people feel stupid if they say no, but trapped if they say yes.

You need just one good question to get a discussion going. Use the questions above as a starting point. Customize them so that they address the particular issues, problems, and concerns faced by your customers. Try them out and fine-tune them as needed.

If your decision maker expresses a concern or indicates an interest in learning more, keep in the investigative mode. The absolute worst thing you can do is to start talking about how great your company is and how you helped another firm solve exactly the same problem and that you'd be delighted to come out to show them how you did this with your latest, greatest offering that is second to none on the marketplace.

Get the point? That's pitching. It's self-serving. It's about you selling. Stop that behavior at once or you'll create resistance.

EXTEND THE DISCUSSION

To have a positive business-to-business discussion, plan additional questions ahead of time. Specifically, you want to:

- explore the decision maker's answers in more depth,
- learn about what they've already tried to do to solve the problem or achieve the goal,
- understand what they perceive the impact to be on their business, and
- determine the priority status of the issue.

In short, be interested in their business. Be curious. If you hear, "We're not thrilled with our current supplier," find out why. Discover the problems they're having. Find out the ramifications of these problems on their business. Resist the temptation to jump in right away with how much better your company is in this area.

If you hear, "Our last initiative in this area wasn't as successful as we'd hoped," find out why they were disappointed. Ask about what went wrong and about the other areas that were impacted because of how they were doing things.

If you hear, "We're concerned that our current processes may not be sufficient to achieve our objectives," find out why they're worried. Ask about their methodology and its shortfalls. Learn more about their business direction, objectives, and critical success factors. Curiosity is good!

How Long Should You Talk?

Continue the call as long as you're having a good discussion. With many prospects, you can sense that time is limited. After you've piqued their interest and asked a few questions, you can tell they're ready to move on. If so, then it's time to draw the conversation to a close.

But if busy corporate decision makers are willing to talk with you for half an hour, that means they're really interested. Truthfully, the only way you keep them engaged is by talking about their business, their concerns, their goals, and their challenges. Also feel free to share how you're helping related customers solve near-identical situations and the results they've attained.

Don't get into a product dump. The temptation can be great. In fact, it may even overcome you. Before you know it, you'll be talking about your latest gizmo or incredible methodologies. Stay away from it.

Close Gently

When you feel like decision makers are interested, that's a good time to suggest the logical next step, the one you've determined prior to placing the call. Here are several ways you can easily, gently advance the sales process:

> "It sounds like what we do could potentially make a difference for your organization. Let's set up a time to get together to explore this in more depth. Is there anyone else you think should be included in the meeting?"

> "If your situation is like my other customers', you could be spending up to 39 percent more than you need to in this area. That's big dollars we're talking about. How about scheduling a meeting with a few others in your group who deal with this issue all the time so we can find out?"

> "With your company's aggressive growth goals, it's going to be a challenge in the upcoming year. I have some ideas I'd like to share with you that could help you get there—on time and within budget. Let's set up a follow-up phone call to talk about this when we both have more time."

Notice how gentle these closing statements are. They simply reiterate a valid business reason for getting together—on the phone or in person—and suggest what could come next. It's like you're talking to a peer.

You're probably thinking that this all sounds too low key to be effective. Your perception of sales has been jaded by observing the very worst in this profession, the manipulative hucksters who don't get into big companies.

To be irresistible to corporate decision makers you simply need to keep your focus on their business issues and challenges. It's all about making a difference for them.

KEY POINTS

- Before you call, remind yourself that you have a valid business reason for contacting this decision maker. Get grounded in the feeling that what your firm offers truly does make a difference.
- Call your lowest priority prospects first. This gives you a chance to warm up, get in the groove, and make mistakes where it doesn't count as much.
- Avoid speaking to a distracted decision maker. Find out right away if your timing is bad, and, if so, suggest an alternative time.
- Establish your credibility immediately. Show that you've done your homework on the prospect's company or have worked with similar firms.
- Have a conversation with decision makers. Engage them in a dialogue by asking provocative, preplanned questions that pique their curiosity and interest.

17

OVERCOME OBSTACLES, ELIMINATE OBJECTIONS

Even when you've piqued the interest of prospective customers, they still are extraordinarily busy human beings who protect their time zealously. A minute wasted is one they'll never get back. Consequently, they quickly cut to the chase to determine if talking with you is a good investment of their time.

If you're unprepared for the common roadblocks, you get tripped up and dismissed in short order. In truth, the decision maker's comments or objections aren't the issue. The real problem is that *you* didn't anticipate them ahead of time and, thus, were caught off guard. Spur-of-the-moment responses rarely work. And, in many cases, they actually create worse problems for you.

As you already know, I'm a strong advocate of preparation. The sellers who succeed in today's marketplace think things through before they act. They leave little to chance. Because it's relatively easy to anticipate a corporate decision maker's likely responses, you have absolutely no reason to ever be caught in this situation again.

STOP CREATING CUSTOMER OBJECTIONS

By following the guidelines in the previous chapter, you set the stage for a positive and interactive discussion. Your value proposition and focus on business results intrigued your prospective customer. It's a good sign when they say:

- "Hmmm. That's interesting. Tell me more."
- "How do you do that? Can you explain that in more depth?"
- "What exactly does your company do?"

Unfortunately, when most people hear those words, they believe they've been given a license to launch into a pitch, a dreadful and highly contagious mistake made frequently by sellers. On the other end of the phone line, the corporate decision maker rapidly shuts down, thinking: "Another typical self-serving salesperson. How can I quickly get myself out of this mess?"

The moment you pause for a breath, your prospect throws out the zinger, "How much does it cost?"

Gulp! Like nearly all sellers, that's the question you dread the most. Now you're on the defensive because you don't sell the cheapest product, service, or solution in town. You don't want to give out pricing yet, but there you are: stuck, forced to talk about how much it costs before you even understand their needs. In short, you've dug your own grave.

So how do you tackle questions like "What does your company do?" By focusing on the problem and the issues instead of what you sell. When my business was focused on new product launches, here's how I responded to the prospect's "tell me more" request:

> "In most organizations, communication between marketing and sales is sorely lacking at launch time. It's like they're in different worlds. When marketing throws the new product over the wall to the sales force, they forget to toss over the tools that the salespeople need to shorten their sales cycles and keep them in the field selling.
>
> "Despite the high hopes everyone had for the new product, before too long it's pretty evident that the launch goals won't be met.

"So, what do *we* do? We work in the gap between marketing and sales to create the tools and to prepare the sales organization for making highly effective sales calls.

"Let me ask you a question: What are the biggest challenges you're facing in introducing new products to the marketplace?"

Notice that this description never once talks about the offering. It really expands on the problem, thus building credibility. Finally, when you end your overview, don't wait in silence for your prospect's next question. Have one of your own ready to ask—a question that focuses the attention back on their needs, their issues, and their concerns.

Your challenge right now is to write your own response out on paper. Again, focus on the problems you solve, the gaps you close, and the difficulties you overcome in helping prospects achieve their objectives. Don't mention any products by name. Instead, talk about your technology, tools, or processes.

Read your proposed response to your colleagues or share it with friends. Ask them: If I said this to you, how likely would you be to ask me the price or to try to get me off the phone? This is one more thing you need to fine-tune, but it's worth doing because you won't be creating your own obstacles. No one likes to run into roadblocks they built themselves!

DEAL WITH THE REALLY TOUGH OBJECTIONS AND OBSTACLES

Always focus on getting rid of the stumbling blocks before they happen rather than recovering from them after they occur. An ounce of prevention is certainly worth a pound of cure.

Prospective customers have a few tried-and-true brush-offs they use to avoid change of any sort. As has already been explained, most brush-offs occur because the seller teed them up somehow. If you find yourself running into these obstacles and objections time and time again, change what you say. Otherwise you'll keep setting your own traps and falling right into them. Here's how you can handle the most common ones you'll run into.

We're Happy with Our Current Vendor, Services, or Solution Provider

Of course they are. If they weren't, they'd have already switched. While this is the most common obstacle you'll encounter, you, like most sellers, are usually unprepared for it. Wanting to learn more, you might ask:

- Who are you currently using?
- What do you like or dislike about them?
- What would it take to get you to consider other suppliers?
- If we could offer you a better price, would you be interested?

None of these questions are effective. They just dig you a deeper hole as prospects reiterate why they don't want to change. The final question appeals only to price shoppers—not most people's idea of a perfect client.

Most likely you created this obstacle by positioning yourself as a "seller" of specific products or services. They can only say they're happy with their present supplier, if you tell them what you sell. It's clear that you brought up your offering too early.

Before you contact the corporate decision maker, poke around the account to figure out who their current service or product supplier is. Then think about how you might slip in under their radar screen by going after only a small piece of the business. Where might your competitor be weak? Less effective? Snoozing on the job? Expand your thinking to determine possible business problems and their resulting implications.

Then when you call up that very same prospect, you can say, "I've been studying your business . . . In my research I learned that . . . I have some ideas I'd like to discuss with you about how we could (solve a problem or achieve a goal)."

When you use this approach, it's virtually impossible to get the "We're happy" response. It also works well for the "We're not interested in new vendors" or "We don't need any" objections.

What Are You Selling?

Ouch! When you hear this question, rest assured you've sounded like every other poorly trained seller on the planet. This question is an immediate customer reaction to a typical product-focused sales representative "spiel." The reaction is difficult to overcome because the prospects already have put you in the category of a schlocky salesperson who just wants their money. To avoid this trap, rethink what you say at the beginning of the call.

Is recovery possible? Only if you can return the focus to their issues, challenges, goals, initiatives, and bottlenecks. Your quick response needs to be like these:

> "My company helps organizations who are struggling with these types of issues: . . . , . . . , and . . . Based on my work with other firms similar to yours, we've helped them achieve the following results . . . The reason I'm calling is to see if this is something you're interested in learning more about."

> "We work with our clients to make a difference in their business operations—specifically in the areas of solving . . . problems related to (critical business issue). Is this something your organization is concerned about today?"

Once again, by using the guidelines in the previous chapter you could have averted this entire problem. As a seller, you have a choice: figure out how to prevent the problem or be constantly tap dancing around while trying to get off the defensive.

BRUSH OFF YOUR PROSPECT'S BRUSH-OFFS

Discussed below are a number of other common obstacles sellers run into—sometimes because saying them is the nature of the buyer and sometimes because they're true. You need to be prepared to address them or else your sales efforts will be quickly derailed.

Send Me a Brochure

When you hear this, know that you're dealing with really nice people. They don't want to hurt your feelings by telling you to "buzz off," so they feign a modicum of interest. However, most have absolutely no intention of doing anything with your brochure other than throwing it right into the wastebasket.

Prospects ask for brochures only when you have initiated the conversation by talking about your product or service. That's why it's critical that you start off by focusing on solving your customer's business problems or helping them achieve their goals. Then this issue disappears completely.

How can you recover? Be honest and upfront. Say this:

> "When there are so many possible ways to address your current situation, brochures are essentially meaningless. Based on my experience, the only way to know if there's a fit between what we offer and your needs is to investigate things more.
>
> "What I can tell you is this: When we worked with Jetstream Services, we were able to improve their operational efficiency 64 percent in less than six months. This enabled them to significantly reduce the cost of goods sold. If you'd like to learn what it would take to achieve similar results, we should set up a time to talk."

Sending a brochure is a waste of time and effort for everyone involved. That's why this comment needs to be gracefully and graciously deflected back to the real issues at hand. Bring the discussion back to your value proposition. Talk about a customer success story. Share ideas about business improvement. Then offer a logical next step that truly advances the process. The only things I'd ever send a prospect would be success stories, white papers, or articles relevant to their business needs.

We're Too Busy Right Now

If you hear this, it's likely a true statement. But the other truth is that they'll still be too busy in six months or even in a year. So don't ask politely, "When should I call you back, Ms. Bigwig?"

This brush-off requires a bit of provocation—something that's tough to do if you don't know the true value of your offering to their business. That's why understanding your value proposition is so important. If you know the difference your offering makes, then you can confidently say:

"Diane, you know as well as I do that six months from now nothing will be different. You'll still have way too much to do without nearly enough time or resources to get it all done. That's why we need to talk sooner rather than later. Right now your company is pouring money on this problem with little to show for it. I have some ideas on how to eliminate redundancies in your workflow that can make a big difference almost immediately. How about we get together sometime in the next couple of weeks? It'll be worth your time."

You have to be pretty confident in your product or service to be able to respond to a prospective customer this way. But let me tell you, it has high impact. They never hear this from sellers. Most back down immediately. This type of response positions you as an expert—someone who really understands their business.

Think you might have a hard time pulling it off? Practice saying your own version of this comeback until you believe yourself. Sometimes that's what it takes!

You're Too High Priced (Sophisticated, Complicated)

The only sellers who run into this obstacle are from fairly well-known firms. Plus, it's based on perception, not reality. Think for a second, though, about why it came up. Is it possible that you were talking about your products or services too soon again? Of course it is; they caught you!

If you talked about issues like the high cost of employee turnover or knocking six months off their product development cycle, you'd never hear this objection. By making the changes in your opening remarks, you'll find that this comment disappears.

Feel free to treat this obstacle humorously. It's simply intended to get you off the phone and has no other meaning. So you might respond, "Depends on what you're trying to accomplish" or "Compared to what?" After listening to their response, redirect the conversation to a focus on business issues.

You've Got Five Minutes Now—Talk

Buyers who say this have always been the most difficult for me because I prefer establishing a connection first. However, they give you no choice. Their challenge forces you to "net it out" or get hung up on. In a panic, most sellers blurt out a quick summary of their product or service. This reaction invariably leads to a response of "We're not interested."

Don't be cowed by these abrupt buyers who are often trying to intimidate you. Instead, go back to virtually the same response you planned to use when a prospect said, "Tell me more." Avoid talking about your offering or capabilities. Focus your comments on the business problems that you solve for your customers and the results you deliver. You may even want to give an overview of how you've helped a specific client. Tell how they handled things before you worked with them, the business issues you addressed, and how you helped them achieve their goals. If possible, highlight statistics, time frames, dollar savings, and more.

After you share this information, don't wait to see what they say. These people respect sellers who are direct and can hold their own. Throw out a question that forces them to think rather than a question requiring a yes or no response. You might ask, "How big an issue is that for you?" or "How are you handling these problems?" Alternatively, you can boldly go for the close: "I know your company is dealing with the same type of issues. That's why I'm calling to set up a time to get together. When will it work on your calendar?"

There's No Money in the Budget

The truth of the matter is that there's never enough money for everything your prospect needs. Even if something is budgeted, it can easily be chopped when something else takes precedence. Finally, you need to realize that it's your job to help your customers get money in the budget for your offering. Knowing that, you might choose to respond as follows:

"No one ever has enough money in their budget, Gwen. But as I mentioned earlier, we helped a high tech firm just like yours shrink their feasibility studies from two months down to five days. The orders lost to delays dropped to zero, resulting in millions of dollars in additional sales revenue.

"These kinds of projects are virtually self-funding and pay for themselves within the budgetary cycle. Let's get together to talk now about how we can help your firm in this area."

Once again, you can only feel confident saying this if you know that what you offer makes a difference to your customers. You won't know if you don't ask.

Sometimes there truly isn't money in the budget for this fiscal year. Nothing you can say or do will change it. If that's the case, you need to meet the decision maker *before* the budget is set to ensure it gets included. Here's how you might address this for the next year:

"From working with other big companies like yours, I know that budgets are determined four to six months prior to the end of the year. I also know that our solutions have a strong return on investment (ROI). As I said in my letter to you, some of our clients have increased Web site conversion ratios by 267 percent in just three months.

"Let's get together to see if what we do is a good fit for your company. Then, if it makes sense, you can include it in your budget for the upcoming year."

Understanding your value proposition from the core of your being gives you the strength to deal with these obstacles.

We Have a Long-Term Contract with Our Supplier

A long-term contract is a tough objection because it's often true. In many cases, big companies sign comprehensive bundled contracts with other large suppliers that include a variety of products and services. Your offering may be a significant improvement over what they're using and may even save them tons of money—but they won't budge.

You have a couple of options with the contract objection. You can wait until it's about expired or you can pursue a foot-in-the-door strategy by finding a gap in the competitor's offering and going after business first. Turn this phone call into an information-gathering session and learn as much as you can. Then spend some time brainstorming about where the opportunities might be before you call again. When you make that next call, be sure to focus on the business issues, not the product.

We Work Only with the Approved Vendor List

This brush-off puts you in a real catch-22 unless you understand what's going on. To get on this list, someone needs to champion your inclusion. The company won't consider adding you unless a request is made. The only way to deal with this one is head-on. You might say:

> "Everyone on the Approved Vendor List is there because a sponsor in your company believes their solution is worthwhile. That's why I'm calling you. What we do makes a big difference for our customers. Again, I'd like to suggest we get together to go over the ideas I mentioned earlier."

This comment should defuse this obstacle—especially if you keep your focus on improving the decision maker's business.

There you have it, a whole chapter full of ideas on how to eliminate those stumbling blocks that get in your way to lining up that appointment. Remember, it's much better to prevent these obstacles than to be on the defensive.

Think about the objections you personally encounter on a frequent basis. Analyze what you might be doing to create problems for yourself. You'll be amazed at what you learn.

Write out and practice your responses ahead of time too. The last thing you want to do is deal with them for the first time when you have a real hot prospect on the phone—especially if this person works at a big company.

KEY POINTS

- Most customer objections are created unintentionally by sellers who focus too much on talking about their offering rather than the business results it provides.

- Don't be blindsided by common obstacles that customers present. Think about them ahead of time and plan your responses.
- When customers say, "Tell me more," don't launch into an overview of your product or service. Instead, expand your discussion of the business problem, its impact on the organization, and the value of solving it.
- To avoid "We're happy with our present supplier" objections, demonstrate your knowledge of your customers' businesses and bring them ideas on how your firm can make a difference.
- Challenge customer brush-offs, such as "Send me a brochure" or "There's no money in the budget," with quiet, but confident statements that keep the opportunity alive. Don't be easily dismissed.

18

TURN GATEKEEPERS INTO GATE OPENERS

When you're trying to get into a big company—especially at the executive level—you sometimes encounter a person who screens access to the decision maker. This gatekeeper—whose job title might be executive assistant, administrative aide, or executive secretary—is a highly trusted advisor to the person you want to meet.

Gatekeepers are intimately aware of the company's goals and objectives as well as key business initiatives and priorities. Most importantly, from your perspective, gatekeepers zealously protect their bosses from unnecessary interruptions to their calendars. They dread the thought of their boss saying, "What were you thinking when you transferred that call to me? Don't ever let any of those self-serving salespeople through again!"

As a result, they become highly skilled at sorting out the lightweight sales "pitchers" from those who demonstrate the knowledge and expertise to make a difference for their organization. As a seller, it feels like you're being grilled by them—and you are! Your challenge is to convince the gatekeeper to let you through, *without* talking about your products, services, or solutions.

Once again, it's imperative to prepare for these inevitable scenarios. But you need to also think about going beyond just "getting through." Gatekeepers are incredible fountains of knowledge about their corporations. By enlisting their help, they can be an incredible asset to you.

HOW NOT TO TREAT A GATEKEEPER

Many sales books have been written about how to sneak past the gatekeeper to get access to the boss. For the most part, they suggest a bunch of slimy techniques that you probably would feel lousy implementing anyway.

But because I'm not one to leave things to chance, let me iterate some basic no-no's regarding how you should never interact with these gatekeepers:

- *Never lie or jade the truth.* While this seems obvious, it's amazing how many people use the "Ms. Bigshot said I needed to talk with your boss" line when they've simply been referred there to get a question answered. When the truth ultimately surfaces, the seller's integrity is always diminished.
- *Never use intimidation tactics.* Some sellers treat the gatekeeper like a peon to be dismissed. They may say, "This is a matter of importance that can only be discussed with Mr. Biggie. Please put me through." Being arrogant immediately lands you on the gatekeeper's "do not help" list.
- *Never treat them like they're stupid.* In their relentless drive to speak to decision makers, some sellers treat gatekeepers as if they're ignoramuses. When these sellers are asked, "What is this call in regards to?", they respond: "It's far too complex to discuss with someone other than Ms. Bigshot. Please put me through." While this may work once, it destroys the hope of any future assistance.
- *Never be evasive.* Gatekeepers are experts at sniffing out sellers. If you don't answer their questions straight up, the likelihood of getting through is slim to none. They want to know who you are, what company you're from, and why their boss should talk to you. Fail to address those concerns satisfactorily and you won't get through.

Don't let anyone tell you that those slippery techniques work like a charm. While they may get you through to the decision maker one time, the way you talked to the gatekeeper will come back to bite you in the end. It's never worth it to be disrespectful.

Gatekeepers are intelligent, talented people, often at the pinnacle of their careers. With all the corporate downsizings in the last decade and the increased popularity of voice mail, very few executives still have their own personal executive assistant. The few who remain take pride in their jobs and know they wield a great deal of power.

Golden **R**ule

Treat gatekeepers with as much respect as you would decision makers.

It's the right thing to do. Plus, it helps you with your sales initiative at the very same time.

Treat Gatekeepers as Colleagues

If you believe that what you sell truly makes a difference to an organization, then you are already aligned with the gatekeeper's objective. Your challenge then is simply to help the gatekeeper understand why you need to talk to or meet with their boss. They have their antennas up at all times and are acutely tuned in to the language of a salesperson. If you slip into that mode even one little bit, they'll block you from getting in.

When gatekeepers screen phone calls for their bosses, they want to know who you are, why you're calling, and if the decision maker is expecting to hear from you. These are the questions you need to be ready to answer.

Fortunately, everything you've learned about talking to decision makers applies to gatekeepers as well. Remember, it's not about your product, service, or solution. They're only tools to achieve specific business results. That's where you need to keep your focus at all times. The quiet confidence you have in the value of your offering needs to shine through as well.

A typical interchange with an executive-level screener might begin like this.

Gatekeeper:	"Mr. Vice President's office. May I help you?"
Seller:	"This is Pat Trenton from SureFire Consulting. I'd like to speak with Jack please."
Gatekeeper:	"What is this in regards to?"

Never be surprised by this question. Because it gets asked every single time, be prepared with your response. Guess what—you already know what to say. That's right. Use virtually the same words you would use if the decision maker picked up the phone. In short, here's the process you can use:

1. Establish your credibility by referencing the person who referred you, the research you've done, or the *triggering event* that occurred.
2. Demonstrate your positive intentions by sharing your value proposition, highlighting key issues they're facing, results your customers have attained, or the valuable information you possess.
3. Suggest that you believe the decision maker would be interested in learning more about the difference you could potentially make for the company.

Here's how the above conversation might play out if the seller observed these guidelines:

Seller:	"When your company issued its third quarter results last week, your CEO talked about the intense competition in the consumer goods market sector and the critical need for new, highly differentiated products."
Gatekeeper:	"Yes."
Seller:	"At SureFire, we help R&D groups create breakthrough product ideas and quickly evaluate market feasibility. One of our recent clients realized sales increases of 22 percent last year from a product that wasn't even a figment of their imagination only seven months earlier.
	"I thought Jack would be interested in learning more. So if you could put me through, I'd appreciate it."

When gatekeepers recognize that your focus is on *their* priority business concerns, they become your ally. Even when they ask if their boss knows you and your response is, "No. That's why I'm calling," it doesn't matter. Now it's simply a matter of finding a time that works for both of you.

Other responses to the gatekeeper's "What is this in regards to?" question could be variations of any of these phrases:

> "I'm calling because I'd like to talk with Ms. Bigshot about some of the challenges your organization is facing related to . . . "

> "I was talking to Cal Conrad in your corporate R&D department. He suggested I speak to your boss."

> "I have some ideas I'd like to run by Mr. Biggie regarding how your company can . . . "

If you've done your homework and have a valid business reason for meeting with the decision maker, the doors of the corporate world swing open for you. When you become allies in your quest to help the decision maker, gatekeepers turn into gate openers.

ENLIST THE SUPPORT OF GATEKEEPERS

Sometimes it's a good idea to initiate contact with a gatekeeper *before* you're ready to talk with the decision maker. Why? Because you need more information to know if an opportunity exists for your offering. If that's your situation, call the decision makers during hours when they're most likely to be in meetings. When you get voice mail, listen for the instructions to get transferred to the gatekeeper. If you don't hear any, try "0" or "#".

When the gatekeeper answers, engage him or her in a discussion. Make sure to introduce yourself and ask for help. Again, don't forget to position the value of your company. When you get the gatekeeper's go-ahead, feel free to ask your questions. Here's an example of what this conversation might look like:

Seller:	"This is Alex Vincent from Egocentric Web Design. I'm hoping you can help me. I have a few questions." (pause)
Gatekeeper:	"Sure."
Seller:	"And with whom am I speaking?"
Gatekeeper:	"Emily Murphy. I'm Ms. Bigshot's executive assistant."
Seller:	"Thanks, Emily. We help retailers convert their online shoppers into buyers. Some of our clients were letting millions of dollars slip away each month due to abandoned shopping carts. Could you help me understand where this issue is right now on your firm's priority list?"

Please notice how the seller asked for the gatekeeper's name right away. This is important because it's respectful and honoring. At the end of any conversation, make sure you have the name written in your notes and spelled correctly. You may also want to get the gatekeeper's e-mail address. That way you can send messages to the gatekeeper which, if they are deemed acceptable, will be forwarded on to the boss.

LEARN FROM GATEKEEPERS

Gatekeepers possess insightful insider information about a variety of topics. Establishing relationships with them enables you to learn about initiatives, priorities, politics, current vendors, shifting focuses, and more. Because helpful gatekeepers can be a gold mine, you'll want to be prepared to ask more than one question. For example, you might ask:

- Do you know if this is an issue Ms. Biggie is concerned about right now?
- Where do the challenges with . . . fit in the priority scheme?
- When do you expect that attention will turn to . . . direction?
- Who else in the organization is involved in this initiative?
- Before I speak with Mr. Bigshot, who else can I talk to that could give me a better understanding of your organization's objectives and challenges?

- Who would I talk to in the company to find out how you're handling things in this area?
- What is the relationship between your area and . . . ?
- How does your boss like to handle challenges like this?
- What's the best way to get a hold of the boss?

Every single time you talk to a gatekeeper, you have an opportunity to learn more. As I build my relationships with gatekeepers, I learn about what's changing in the company and what's going on in their lives as well as in the lives of their bosses. They let me know the best time to reach the boss. And, if I'm having trouble catching the decision maker, they may even go the extra mile and make special arrangements for me to connect with this person.

In one case, the gatekeeper had tried several times to hook me up with her boss who always seemed to have last minute things come up. On the Friday that he was "for sure" going to be in the office at 2 PM, my message again rolled to voice mail. This time when I spoke to the gatekeeper, I said jokingly, "Does this man really exist?"

She laughed and said, "Yes, but he's impossible to keep track of. Let me give you his cell phone number. He's at the airport right now, waiting to catch a plane."

It's not too often that you get the cell phone number of the president of a company. But my relationship with the gatekeeper made it possible.

Always make sure you treat gatekeepers with the utmost respect. That means being respectful of their time too. They have a great deal of responsibility and are not interested in chitchatting with callers. Have your questions prepared in advance; make sure they're well thought out and to the point.

Make sure to thank gatekeepers for any guidance you receive. Because they don't have to help you, show your appreciation. Never forget that they can make or break you within an account. If they feel good about working with you, they'll do everything they can to get you a spot on the decision maker's calendar. If not, they'll block your efforts at every turn.

KEY POINTS

- Gatekeepers are highly skilled at sorting out product-focused sales pitchers from business professionals focused on making a quantifiable difference.
- Never use slippery, sleazy, or manipulative techniques on gatekeepers. While they may get you in the door, they'll hurt you in the long run.
- Be prepared for the common question, "What is this in regards to?" Your response to it determines if the gatekeeper lets you through to the decision maker.
- Always treat gatekeepers as respected colleagues. Help them understand why their bosses will benefit from speaking with you.
- Gatekeepers are invaluable sources of insider information. To learn more about their companies, their bosses, and even potential opportunities, develop a positive relationship with them.

19

KEEP THE
CAMPAIGN ALIVE

At this point, you're probably wondering just how long you should keep going with your account entry campaign before calling it quits. Remember, it takes at least seven to ten contacts before you start registering on a prospective client's Richter scale. Stop before that and all your efforts to get into the big company are wasted.

Your real challenge is to stay fresh throughout the campaign. That's going to require you to constantly be on your toes, thinking creatively about what you might do next. Many sellers aren't used to this way of working with clients. They want to operate on automatic pilot, without engaging their brain in the process. Being good at selling requires constant thinking.

STAY IN TOUCH WITHOUT
SOUNDING DESPERATE

Over the years, you wouldn't believe how many people have confided in me that they're terrified of sounding totally pathetic or needy when they recontact prospective buyers. They're anxious about calling people back because they need the business so badly, but they don't want to convey the impression that they're desperate for it. This feeling frequently translates into sales behaviors that sellers interpret one way, yet are seen totally differently by corporate decision makers.

To overcompensate for their fears, anxieties, and doubts about if anything is happening at the account, many sellers move into "nice" mode. When they pick up the phone to get back to prospective buyers, suddenly their good sense flies out the window and they leave messages that sound like this:

> "Mr. Biggie, Dave Murakami calling. I left you a voice mail recently about how my company, Swift Services, helps speed up manufacturing processes. I'm just checking in with you to see how everything is going in your plant and if you need anything that we might offer. If you're interested in learning more about our services, I'd be glad to come out and talk with you or send you a brochure. My number is . . . "

Wait a minute! What just happened here? The seller got nervous and started jabbering. Suddenly he's "just checking in," wondering how "everything is going," and if his services are needed. In his attempt to be nice, nonchalant, and conversational, everything Dave said sounds disgustingly salesy to corporate decision makers.

Buyers hate hearing this message too: "I was just checking in to see if you got the letter I sent you last week and if you might have any questions about it." Whether you leave that on a voice mail or say it in person, it makes you sound like a postal inspector—not a professional in your field.

Other phrases that are huge turnoffs and should be avoided at all costs include:

- "I'm calling to see if you need any . . . I don't want to bother you, but I'm trying to help out."
- "I wanted to keep in touch to see if you might be ready to do something regarding . . . "
- "I'm wondering how things are going with that (*triggering event*) and if you might be looking for resources soon."
- "I was just checking in to see if anything has changed."

All these "no-brainer" follow-up messages immediately dissipate any credibility you built up in earlier, well-planned contacts. To avoid sounding pathetic, you must always have a valid business reason for calling each and every time. Specifically, you will want to:

- stress a different aspect of your value proposition;
- share the results another one of your customers attained; and
- bring your prospect interesting news about the industry, their customers, their competitors, or changing legislation.

When you do this, you never sound desperate. Instead, you sound like a valuable resource and a person of interest. If you're constantly adding value in your phone calls, mailings, and e-communications, there's no need to worry about being perceived as a nuisance or pest.

As a guideline, I suggest that making one contact every week or two is quite appropriate. Beyond that, it's hard for decision makers to connect the dots between your "touches." There are times when you might want to be more frequent in your attempts to get in. If you note the occurrence of a *triggering event* that has immediate negative business ramifications related to your offering, then don't worry about being a pest. Someone in that company may be desperate for your help.

WHAT TO DO WHEN DECISION MAKERS CONTACT YOU

While we may dream of the day when prospective customers call us back, it can also be very disconcerting because it happens so seldom.

There have been several times in my sales career when I've been on a prospecting binge. My pipeline was running dry and I needed new customers. I made numerous phone calls into my targeted accounts, trying to track down the decision makers so I could get my foot in the door. I left messages everywhere. No one ever called me right back.

Then, a few days later when I'd be totally immersed in another project, the phone would ring. I'd absentmindedly pick it up and say, "Hello. This is Jill."

Invariably, the voice on the other end responded, "Jill. This is Mike. I'm returning your call."

Mike? I'd think. Mike who? And from what company? My mind would go blank. I'd desperately rack my brain as I mumbled, "Mike! Thanks for getting back to me."

But then I'd be stuck. I didn't have a clue what company he was from. I had no idea what message I had left. I didn't know if he was the decision maker I was trying to reach or the friend of a friend with whom I was networking.

I can assure you that there's nothing more humbling and humiliating than having to say, "Mike. I'm sorry, but I can't place who you are." Your credibility instantly evaporates. Despite all the precall planning you've done to get this far, you look like an idiot. (Remember, this is the voice of experience talking!)

Set Up Your "Memory" System

The first thing you need to do is set up a system to minimize the chances of this happening. Earlier we talked about the importance of focusing on a few targeted accounts. Pursuing business with ten big companies is more than enough for most sellers. Going after hundreds of prospects concurrently turns you into a basic peddler. There's only so much you can keep in your head at any one time.

There are multiple ways to set up systems that work. The key is to find a "memory" system that works well for *you.*

Some people love contact management software and use it religiously. They enter in every bit of information about the account, the decision makers, messages they've left, e-mails they've sent, and other pertinent data. When a decision maker calls them, they quickly access their database to find the relevant facts. With PDAs, this information is totally portable too.

Other people still like paper filing systems. If this is your preference, make sure to keep all your active prospecting files handy so you can use them at a moment's notice. Over the years, I've found it helpful to write the contacts' names and numbers on the outside of these folders so I don't have to go digging through them when I'm under pressure.

I personally like to keep a one-page sheet listing everyone's name, title, company, and phone number sitting on the top of my desk too. I leave a little space to jot down something to jog my memory about my last contact.

And last, but certainly not least, use caller ID if you have it. Before you pick up the phone, check out who is calling. Sometimes that's all you need to do to get yourself grounded.

On Being Caught Unawares

The last thing you want to do is enter into a discussion with a prospective client when you're still trying to figure out who in the world you're talking to. Let me suggest a strategy that can buy you a few minutes to regroup and get your head thinking straight.

If you're ever caught in that embarrassing position where you don't know who's on the phone, say, "Mike. Thanks for calling. Can I get back to you in just a few minutes? I'm right in the middle of something."

Nearly everybody will agree. They know how distracting it is to be interrupted while they're working. If they say that they'll be tied up shortly, then all you have to do is figure out a time that works for both of you.

Make sure you follow up your initial call-back request with this phrase: "Can you give me your number again? I don't have it handy."

That's how you get the information you need to figure out who you're talking with. If you're still confused, call back the number but change the last digit. You'll end up speaking with someone else in the firm (or their voice mail) and can find out that way.

Then, before you make that return call, review your notes and get yourself grounded in what you want to say or discuss with the decision maker. You don't want to sound like a stumblebum. You want to come across as the true professional you are.

PREPARE LIKE A PRO FOR CALLBACKS

To be your best when someone calls you back, it's imperative to understand what a decision maker needs from you at that moment in time.

Your heart may be racing a zillion miles per hour. Your mouth may go dry from a bad case of the nerves. You may feel like shouting "Alleluia" at the same time your knees are quaking.

But the person on the other end of the line needs to sense that you are calm, cool, and collected—the exact opposite of how you feel. That's why you need to plan how to handle the call-back situation before it occurs. Otherwise, I guarantee you'll say something like this:

> "Ms. Bigshot. Thank you so much for getting back to me. I really, really appreciate it. I've wanted to talk with you for a long time and I know how busy you are. I'm honored that you've called me back."

Feeling elated and giddy is normal. Sounding that way is detrimental to your sales efforts. This babbling giddiness positions you as a lightweight in your business. While you may think you sound nice and respectful, you sound amateurish.

People in big companies don't want to deal with rookies. They want to work with talented, knowledgeable professionals. Your entire mental framework must be that you're dealing with a peer. This doesn't mean that you're necessarily on an equal level with the decision maker. But it does mean that you know that your company offering provides significant value to customers.

When someone calls you back, your immediate comments must bridge the gap between the previous contact (e.g., voice mail, e-mail, letter) and today. For example, you might say:

> "Bob. Thanks for getting back to me. As I mentioned in the letter I sent, we're doing lots of work right now with online retailers to significantly increase their conversion rates. Because you're calling me back, that must be something on your priority list right now. Right?" (pause)

> "Tony. Thanks for returning my call. As I mentioned in my voice mail, I understand your company is introducing some important new products this year. We help companies shrink time-to-revenue at launch time, and I wanted to find out if this is a concern of yours right now." (pause)

As you can see, these responses specifically connect the reason for the initial call with today's conversation. They're focused on issues—not products, services, or solutions. Essentially, they're a reiteration of your value proposition.

Please notice their conversational nature as well. They're easy to say and short—about 15 seconds maximum. Additionally, the last line is specifically designed to engage your prospective customer in a conversation about their issues and challenges. After you say it, be quiet and let your customer talk.

Now that you've started the dialogue, you can move back into the call plan you created to reach a potential buyer on the phone. When they phone you back, all you need is this transition and then you're all set.

WHEN DO YOU QUIT TRYING TO GET IN?

How long do you keep the campaign active before you decide to invest your time in other opportunities that may have more upside potential? As I said earlier, you need between seven to ten contacts to become a recognized entity. Assuming that you contact the account once every ten days, your campaign could go on for three to four months.

If you haven't made any inroads at the end of that period, you need to look elsewhere. But don't remove this big company from your list altogether. Even when your campaign is perfectly executed, there could be innumerable reasons why it's not working out right now that are entirely out of your control.

Find a way to keep in touch once a quarter. That way you keep yourself on their radar screen without being obtrusive. Send interesting articles to the decision makers. E-mail them informative Web site links. Make a phone call sharing important industry trends. Invite them to an upcoming Webinar put on by your firm.

Unless you're specifically told never to contact the person again, don't completely give up. It's highly likely that it's just a matter of priorities. Other things are simply more important to work on or resolve at this moment in time. By keeping in touch, when the time does come to tackle the issues your company addresses, you will have top-of-mind awareness.

KEY POINTS

- To avoid sounding pathetic on follow-up calls, don't ever say something lame like, "I'm just checking in." These calls are as important as your initial one and require just as much planning.
- To generate interest over time, stress different aspects of your value proposition, share results your customers have attained, or tempt your prospect with new information.
- If a decision maker contacts you when you're not anticipating it, it's important to have time to gather your thoughts. Thank him or her for calling and ask if you can call back in a few minutes.
- Always bridge your contacts with decision makers. Reference key points in your letter or voice mail to get them grounded, then ask a question.
- If you've contacted decision makers between seven to ten times over several months with no success, then move them to a quarterly follow-up schedule. Their lack of interest is usually a matter of corporate priorities.

Part Five

ADVANCE THE SALE

20

PLAN AN AWESOME FIRST MEETING

Whenever you set up a meeting with a corporate decision maker, you deserve a round of applause. Make sure you take time to pat yourself on the back for a job well done. Your accomplishment sets you apart from all those other sellers who are still scratching their heads trying to figure out how to get in.

As you prepare for this upcoming meeting—whether it's a phone conversation or an in-person appointment—remember that people who work for big companies generally feel swamped, overwhelmed, and stressed out. They're expected to achieve aggressive goals on limited budgets and minimal resources. Time is their most precious commodity. You've been allotted a slot in their busy schedule because the decision maker believes you can either solve a problem or help achieve a desired business result.

When you're talking to them, that's what will be on your prospective customers' mind. Not your product. Not your service or technology or solution. Only their business issues. Your entire account entry campaign focused on business, and business is what your prospect expects to talk about when you get together. If you don't deliver on this promise, you won't have another chance.

Your challenge now is to transform this opportunity into a business relationship. Yet you only have a short time in which to make this happen.

AVOID DIARRHEA OF THE MOUTH

If you're like most sellers, intellectually you know it's important to focus on your customer and to ask questions about their objectives, issues, and concerns. But inside, you're in turmoil because you have all this information you "need" to share.

"Besides," you may think, "what if I don't tell them about everything we can do? If I focus on one thing only, what if that thing is not what they need right now?"

Many sellers, fearful that they'll only get this one chance to demonstrate their expertise or razzle dazzle their prospect, make the classic mistake of talking too much on sales calls. Research shows that the less time sellers have with a prospective buyer, the more likely they are to spend it in a pitching mode.

Don't let this fear get in the way of your success. Sales pitches don't work. If you're overcome by diarrhea of the mouth on your first call, you're in trouble. Yet, most sellers aren't even aware of it when they switch into this mode. They have absolutely no idea they're blabbing on and on about their offering. Instead they see themselves as simply responding to questions posed by interested prospects. This delusion leads to disaster before they even know it.

When this happens, prospective customers typically react by saying things like:

- "How much does it cost?" If they ask this question before you have discussed their needs, the end is in sight. No matter what the price, it's too much; you're on the defensive trying to justify value.
- "Can it do . . . ?" Questions about what your product or service can do are asked to rule out options. Customers would rather stay with the status quo than change. If they uncover even one trivial "glitch," you may be done.
- "Very interesting. I bet you'll sell a lot." While unsaid, this statement really ends with "but not here." These customers are being nice but want you out of their office. They think you're only interested in a sale—not helping their business.

If you try to convince prospective customers that your products, services, or solutions are what they need, you're digging your own grave.

By showing them everything in your goody bag, you sound just like a peddler—the type of salesperson you detest the most.

HOW TO CONVERSE WITH PROSPECTIVE CUSTOMERS

Good selling is about creating conversations with decision makers, not pitching. It's about focusing on their business only. Remember, your offering is only a tool to help them achieve their desired outcomes.

Your prospective clients must know from the onset that your one and only goal is to help them remove obstacles or impediments to reaching their business objectives. Maintaining this focus is the best way to lay the groundwork for a mutually beneficial relationship.

So if you can't discuss your products, services, or solutions, what can you talk about? Go back to your account entry campaign to find the answers.

Discuss Business Results

If you focused on your value proposition or shared a customer success story to get your foot in the door, your prospect wants to find out how you helped other firms achieve these same results.

Listen carefully to me now. Rather than telling about your process, capabilities, or technology, which you're probably dying to do, be ready to share the following information at the beginning of your meeting:

- How customers did things prior to working with your firm
- The problems they encountered in their operations
- The business ramifications of these problems
- The specific value and business outcomes they've realized as a result of your relationship

When decision makers ask about "how" you did this, be brief and succinct. Simply say something like this: "We put together a customized plan that really addressed their very specific needs and issues." Or, you could say this: "They utilized one of our new products to get these results. However, at this point I would need to know more to determine if that would be the right option for your firm."

> Your goal is to quickly transition to questions so you can learn more about your prospect.

Now move into asking questions. That's the end of your talking for a while. A conversation is a two-way street. It's time to get the decision maker involved.

Expand Insightful Ideas

If you enticed your prospect to meet with you because you shared an insightful idea, focus on that idea when you meet. However, rather than making it sound like your idea is the perfect solution, position it as a possibility that needs to be explored in more depth. Here's how you tee that up at the beginning of the meeting:

- Mention the research you did prior to initiating contact.
- Point out what you've learned from working with other similar clients. Focus on their business issues, critical success factors, and obstacles to success.
- Bring up what you discovered about the prospect's business in terms of likely problem areas, bottlenecks, or work arounds.
- Share ideas about how other customers successfully tackled these same challenges and the results they achieved.
- Emphasize that you can't be sure that these same ideas would work for this particular client, but you felt it was worth exploring their situation in more depth.

Don't get sucked into a discussion of your products, services, or solutions. You goal is to start a conversation about their business. After sharing your idea, transition quickly to questions.

Provide Important Information

Big companies are always interested in information about their industry, marketplace, customers, and competitors. If you dangled the fact that you possess some of this vital information to get into the big company, then that's where your conversation starts. To get the discussion underway, you'll want to:

- Establish the context for the information you'll be sharing: Where did you get this info? Who's it from? Things like that.
- Review the information with the client. It's often helpful to have graphs, charts, white papers, or articles to solidify your message and increase its perceived value.

After you've shared the information, again move into questions as soon as possible. If you're in a presentation mode the whole time, you're not having a conversation. The lack of interaction puts you at an extreme disadvantage in terms of advancing to the logical next step. Also make sure the information you share is not a thinly veiled sales pitch.

ENGAGE IN QUESTIONABLE PRACTICES

What most sellers don't realize is that the only way to achieve the status of a trusted advisor is by asking pointed questions. Not by blabbing everything they know. Not by telling customers what changes need to be made. Not by talking endlessly about their unique capabilities or technology.

Well-planned, thought-provoking questions lead to strong relationships with corporate buyers—and ultimately to lots of business. Asking insightful, customer-focused questions enables you to:

- *Demonstrate your positive intentions.* Questions show customers you're concerned about their business, not just getting the order.
- *Increase your credibility.* Well-thought-out questions make you appear significantly more competent, especially if they're framed with your industry, market, competitive, or customer knowledge.

- *Help customers think and assess.* This is highly valued by decision makers who have little time in their day to analyze and strategize. They appreciate questions that give them fresh perspectives on their challenges and issues.
- *Uncover and develop needs.* Asking questions helps you learn about the bottlenecks, frustrations, and aggravations decision makers face on a daily basis. Unless you uncover these problems or issues, your customers will stay with the status quo.
- *Shape the right solution for your customers.* While this isn't something you'll do on the first call, it's on your mind for future meetings when a proposal is needed.

Plan your questions ahead of time. If you don't, you have better than 90 percent chance of reverting to that disgusting "pitching" behavior when you meet with prospective clients. Why? Because your brain can't think of good questions at the same time it's listening to your customer. You'll get nervous. Then you'll start to talk, then jabber. Pretty soon you'll be out of control.

It's absolutely imperative to develop a list of ten questions to take with you into the meeting. You might think that this makes you look like a rookie, but real pros do it all the time.

Neil Rackham's groundbreaking sales research showed that the ability to ask good questions was the single biggest differentiator between top sellers and average sellers. When top sellers learned about problems or concerns, they kept asking questions to discover the business ramifications and the value of making a change.

In contrast, the moment average sellers heard their prospect express a difficulty or dissatisfaction, they quickly jumped in with their solutions.

GUIDELINES FOR GOOD QUESTIONING

When you first meet with or talk to corporate decision makers, you'll have more questions to ask than can possibly be answered in one meeting. Don't worry. You're building a relationship and will have many opportunities in the future to learn more about your customers.

Find Out about the Current Situation

When you start asking questions, focus on the customer's current situation as it relates to the problems you solve or objectives you can help them achieve. To avoid sounding like a police interrogator, try to create bigger questions that elicit fuller answers.

A few years ago I coached a sales representative who was very excited about a new product his company had introduced. We role-played a call he was going to make the next week at a large corporate account. He asked me a hundred questions in just a few minutes, some of which were:

- What system do you use for this application?
- What software are you using?
- How long have you had it?
- Who do you use for support?
- Where does the information go when you're done with your job?
- What system is that person using?

"Stop," I finally said, putting my hands over my ears. "All you need is one question."

He gave me one of those "yeah-sure" looks.

"Just say to your customer, 'Tell me how the work flows through your operation,'" I said. "When your customer answers, you'll learn what's going on. The rest of your questions will come out during the course of normal conversation."

Also, don't ever ask a question about information that's readily accessible to the public. It makes you look stupid—and that's the last way you want to be perceived.

Get a Handle on Their Problems and Gaps

Ignore this step and you can't sell. If customers are totally happy with the status quo, they have no reason to change. You may feel uncomfortable asking about their problems because you feel it's impolite or too personal.

Get over it. You can't help customers improve their business unless you're willing to be uncomfortable. Selling is not about you. It's about solving current and future problems. If you're truly a customer-focused person, you *must* ask questions about what's wrong.

Questions that uncover problems and gaps have evaluative words in them. Key words to include in problem or gap questions include:

Bottlenecks	Difficulties	Troubles
Challenges	Issues	Dissatisfaction
Barriers	Problems	Changes
Concerns	Improvements	Frustrations

Ask the decision maker questions specifically related to the business problems your offering solves. We talked about this earlier in Chapter 7: Strengthening Your Value Proposition. Look at the problems you listed. Develop questions around these problems to find out if your customer considers them to be significant issues. For example, you might ask questions such as:

- What are your most pressing problems related to . . . ?
- What are the primary challenges you face in growing your business?
- Where do the bottlenecks occur?
- What are the biggest barriers to achieving your goals?
- What improvements are needed to increase your operational efficiency?
- Based on how you're doing things today, what are the biggest concerns?

When customers share their answers, be curious and learn more about their issues. Specifically, you'll want to know why they consider it a problem.

Explore the Business Impact

Whenever you uncover an area of concern related to the solutions you provide, *do not* jump in and start talking about your offering. Instead, keep asking questions that uncover the "ripple effect" of the problems you've discovered.

Again, this was covered in earlier discussions related to your value proposition. Review the business implications of the problems that customers experience when they don't work with your company. Then create insightful questions that engage the decision maker in exploring the consequences of their current methodology.

Key words to include in these questions include *impact, consequences, affect, implications, effect,* and *ramifications.* Examples of questions you might ask include:

- How do these problems impact profitability?
- How does the difficulty with . . . affect (other area)?
- What are the implications for your organization if those problems aren't addressed successfully?
- You mentioned turnover was an issue. How is that impacting your training costs? Hiring costs? Error rate?

Customers like these kinds of questions because they make them think. They also give you lots of good information to build a business case for your offering. Top sellers ask significantly more of these types of questions than average sellers.

Determine the Value of Change

After you've explored the business implications of your customer's problems, it's time to determine the payoff they get from resolving them. When customers answer these questions, they tell you how their business would be better if their problems were resolved. In essence, the customers sell themselves.

Top sellers are extremely proficient at asking these types of questions. Most average sellers rarely ask them. These questions are positive and solution-oriented. Key words to include in these questions are *help, important, value, useful, benefit, assist, aid,* and *worth.* Here are some sample questions you could ask that would help determine the value from your customer's perspective:

- If that problem were solved, what value would it provide to your organization?
- Why is it important for you to fix . . . ?

- Help me understand why cutting turnaround time would benefit your group?
- Are there any other ways it would help?
- What is it worth to you to free up additional space?

After you ask these questions, lean back and listen—even if you're talking to this person on the phone. Keep exploring your customer's answers for as long as you can. Make sure you take good notes too because what you learn can be invaluable.

Good questions are the key to turning merely frustrated prospects into active buyers looking to resolve their problems. Create a list of ten primary questions you want to ask when you talk with corporate decision makers. This list guides you in creating a sales conversation and keeps your focus on your prospective customer—exactly where it belongs.

KEY POINTS

- The biggest mistake made by sellers on initial calls is trying to convince prospective customers of their value by touting their product, service, or solution.
- Maintain a focus on helping your customer remove obstacles to reaching their goals and objectives. Remember, your offering is simply a tool to these end results.
- Begin by giving a brief overview of the business results attained by your customers or sharing an insightful idea. Transition to questions as quickly as possible.
- Insightful questions have a bigger impact on your sales success than any other sales behavior. Plan them ahead of time for maximum impact.
- To engage clients in a discussion, ask questions focused on the challenges, problems, and issues they face. Explore their business impact and the payoff for making a change.

21

DEVELOP AN
UNSTOPPABLE
MOMENTUM

Now that we've explored the essence of your sales conversation with the corporate decision maker, it's time to look at exactly what will transpire during your appointment. Your meeting doesn't start when you get the decision maker on the phone or the moment you walk in the door. It actually begins several days earlier when you develop your game plan.

To be most successful, it's imperative for you to think like your prospective customers think. In most cases, they want to know if you understand their industry, company, issues, and challenges. They want to feel like you care about helping them achieve their goals or solve their problems. You never, ever, convince people of this by talking at them. Only intelligent business-oriented discussions lead to this result.

This type of dialogue doesn't just occur spontaneously. It requires a great deal of thinking before you go in. Every single top seller I know invests significant time in the preparation stage. They know that "winging it" doesn't work with today's corporate buyer.

KNOW WHERE YOU'RE GOING
BEFORE YOU GET THERE

People in big companies seldom, if ever, make snap decisions. It typically takes multiple meetings and phone conversations to solidify your foot-in-the-door contract, project, or order—even if your offering saves them huge amounts of time and money while growing their sales exponentially.

Yet when I ask many sellers what their main objective is for the initial meeting, they tell me, "Get the business." Going into a meeting with this goal is a setup for failure, especially if you use the lame closing techniques promoted by many so-called sales gurus.

Other sellers are much "nicer." Their goal is to gather information; they want to learn more about the company. These sellers hope the decision maker will ask them lots of questions about their offering. Unfortunately, they erroneously believe that if they do a good job describing it, they'll get the business sometime in the foreseeable future.

When selling to big companies, you need to move forward in steps. What exactly are those steps? To find out, analyze the process your customers go through to make a decision. As a seller, you can't short-circuit their decision cycle. You need to align with it, making sure you're doing whatever you can to advance it to the logical next step. That's your responsibility—not your prospective buyers.

Based on my experience in working with business-to-business sales organizations, common logical next steps include:

- *Follow-up conversations with the decision maker.* Often because of time constraints, you will still have much to explore and discuss after your initial contact. It's also likely you'll need some time to think about what you've learned and come back with some ideas.
- *Meetings with the decision maker's colleagues.* Because most corporate buyers involve others in their decisions, you might want to suggest phone or in-person meetings with their colleagues, bosses, subordinates, technical evaluators, users, or financial people.
- *Meetings with your colleagues.* Other people in your own organization can bring significant value to the sales process. You might want to set up a time for a conversation or meeting with your industry specialist, technical expert, executive, or someone else in your company.

What do you do in these follow-up meetings? In the early stages, you may spend quite of bit of time developing an in-depth knowledge of your prospect's situation and challenges. You could be conducting interviews, reviewing records, analyzing methodology, talking with clients, or doing surveys.

As your momentum builds, you may get involved in making presentations, delivering proposals, arranging site visits, or having plan and review meetings.

Your initial meeting is successful only if you end up with a specific outcome that advances your relationship. Before you go into it, know the logical next step you'll propose. Don't worry if you end up with a different progression than you anticipated. Sometimes your prospect's insight into how his company operates can be extremely useful in determining the best next step. To keep the momentum going, get it scheduled on the calendar before you leave. If you don't, it will be virtually impossible to get back in the door—even if they love you!

COMPLETE THE SALES CALL PLANNING GUIDE

Effective meetings with corporate decision makers follow a simple, proven process. Here are the steps to follow to ensure you have a productive first sales call. Please use these steps as guidelines, not absolutes. The time frames below assume a one-hour meeting. And remember, good meetings focus on your prospective customers and what's important to them—not your product, service, or solution. (Note: While it's more likely that your meeting will occur in person, this plan works well for phone meetings as well.)

I. Open the Conversation (5–10 minutes)

Customers from big companies don't have a lot of time for meaningless chitchat and relationship building these days. Be cordial and friendly, but business-focused at all times.

A. *Make the introductions*

Take a few minutes to learn about the decision maker's job and responsibilities. If the decision maker invites others to the meeting, make sure to introduce yourself and learn their names. Find out why they're attending and what interests they have relative to the business issue.

B. *Confirm times and agenda*

Before you get started, double-check to see if times have changed since you set up the meeting. If your customer has to run to an urgent meeting in 30 minutes, you need to adjust your game plan or come back later. Reconfirm the purpose of the meeting also to ensure there are no misunderstandings.

You might say, "As I explained earlier, we work with high-tech firms to increase brand awareness and drive sales. In our time together today, I'd like to give you a little background on how we address these issues, find out what your company is doing in these areas, and see if we have grounds for further discussions. How does that sound?"

Notice the professionalism and leadership in this overview statement. It shows that you have a clear plan for the meeting. Decision makers feel better immediately; they know their precious time won't be wasted.

II. Lead the Discussion (40–45 minutes)

You want to create a dialogue—not make a pitch. Lay the groundwork by sharing information of high interest to your prospects. Then invite them into a discussion by asking questions that make them think.

A. *Set the stage (5 minutes)*

Customers need more grounding about what your company does than the brief one-sentence statement given above. When you arranged the meeting, the decision maker was enticed by something you said.

Now is the opportune time to give a *brief* overview of the *business results* a specific client achieved with your product, service, or solution. Explain the challenge your customers faced, how you helped them, and the results they were able to achieve. You can also share your insightful ideas or go over the important information you brought to the meeting. The previous chapter explains what to do in detail.

B. Transition to questions

As quickly as you can, shift the focus to the decision maker—where it belongs. To do this, simply say, "That should give you a good overview about how we help our customers solve their problems (or achieve their objectives). The most important thing is to find out if this makes sense for your company. In preparing for today's meeting, I noticed that (insert data re: company's direction, *triggering event*, other info uncovered in research). I was wondering how . . . "

Unless you plan your transition, it's sometimes hard to stop talking—especially if you're goaded on by questions from the decision maker. An effective transition is part of your sales call plan.

C. Focus on business issues (35–40 minutes)

Prior to the meeting, develop a minimum of ten insightful, powerful questions you can use to lead a business-focused discussion. Corporate decision makers are always interested in talking about their business. They wouldn't be taking time to meet with you unless they truly wanted help solving their problems or achieving their goals.

Have the questions handy so you can refer to them. If you want, show the client how you've prepared for the meeting—they'll be impressed. But don't give them the list of questions or they'll just rattle off the answers.

Ask your questions in a conversational manner—not like a schoolteacher giving an oral test. Questions build relationships, establish rapport, demonstrate your competence, and show that you care.

Remember, this is a discussion—not a sales pitch. Listen to their answers. Be interested. Learn as much as you can. Take copious notes of everything that's said—not just the parts you find interesting.

Always *lean* back. The moment you move forward, you're pitching. The discussion is over, and the push is on. Your prospect immediately puts up defensive barriers and raises objections. Getting the sale is going to be infinitely harder unless you immediately recover and get back into the discovery mode.

III. Advance the Process (5–10 minutes)

When you focus on questions, your one-hour meeting flies by. Even if the decision maker seems oblivious to the time, it's important not to overstay your welcome. Draw attention to the clock. See if you're invited to stay longer. If not, it's time to wrap up and advance the sales process to the logical next step.

A. *Summarize your understanding*

Because it takes multiple meetings to do business with big companies, on your first call don't try to share everything you know, ask every question you want answered, or hand out every piece of collateral in your briefcase. Instead, show your professional expertise by summarizing what you learned about their critical business issues and the value of resolving them.

Corporate decision makers are also interested in learning more about how you work with customers who had similar problems, what your process was in working with them, and how they benefited from working with your firm.

Do not under any circumstances get into a discussion of your product or service. This will be the hardest thing in the whole world for you to avoid doing, but it's essential. Remember, corporate buyers don't really care about your offering—only what it can do for them. They also realize that in a short one-hour meeting, you can't possibly offer them a well-thought-out solution. They don't expect one.

B. *Suggest the logical next step*

Then, without making a big deal of it, simply recommend a good option to move the process forward. This is the logical next step you were working toward from the onset.

You might say, "Usually when I work with companies on product introductions, the next step is to set up a meeting with the product manager to get a better understanding of the launch plans already in place and where gaps might exist. Can we get a meeting set up with this person in the next couple weeks?"

If you've had a good discussion, it's highly likely that your prospect will have already suggested a next step. If so, great! Get it on the calendar. If your prospect missed an important step, offer it up as another idea: "Ms. Biggie, I'll get going on your recommendation right away. Also, based on my experience, we need to talk with the IT department as well. Can we get that set up too?"

Ending meetings in this manner advances the sales process to its next logical step. It's honest and full of integrity. It's just simply suggesting the next logical thing that you both need to do to determine if your offering is a good fit for their business.

Use Tool 9: Sales Call Planning Guide in Appendix A to help you plan for your upcoming sales meetings.

MAKE SURE YOU'RE SET UP FOR SUCCESS

The more you can do to ensure everything goes well in your meeting the better. Being proactive helps eliminate problems and prevents you from wasting time. Here are a few more suggestions to make your meeting a success:

- *Call to confirm your appointment.* Yes, you risk having to reschedule, but that's better than getting there and meeting with a distracted decision maker. When you place the call, don't just say you're checking in to make sure you're still on at 10 AM.

  Follow that statement with something enticing such as, "I've been doing some additional research on . . . and have some ideas I want to share with you." It's essential to reaffirm that your meeting will be a valuable use of this person's time.
- *Send a preliminary agenda.* Decision makers from big companies like to know the focus of the meeting prior to your arrival. Partly

it's so they know their time won't be wasted. Pulling together a simple agenda is a good discipline for you as well because it forces you to prepare for the meeting in advance. Send the agenda by e-mail, fax, or hard copy.

- *Don't bring any brochures.* If you do, you won't be able to resist pulling them out. Once you do that, forget it. You've been relegated to a product-pushing salesperson whose only interest is in your own pocketbook. If you're asked about brochures, just say, "I never bring collateral along when I first meet with someone. My entire focus in on your business issues and challenges. If there's a good fit, we can talk specifics later."

WHAT DO YOU DO IF . . . ?

While you'd like to think that everything would go as planned, sometimes you run into some glitches that you haven't anticipated. Discussed below are the most frequent questions I get asked, along with a few ideas to help you deal with these unexpected situations.

What Do You Do If They Really, Really Want to Talk about Your Product or Service?

Find out immediately if this is something they'll be making a decision on in the upcoming weeks. If they haven't committed to making a change, then it's likely you've created this situation yourself by talking about your offering too much.

Very politely say, "Mr. Biggie, we've been talking about my offering too much. The real issue is if it will help you achieve your objectives. That's something we've barely touched on. I've prepared some questions that can help us determine if it's a good business decision for your firm." Then, ask a question.

When this meeting is over, try to figure out what you did to create this scenario because it's a problem usually induced by the sales representative.

What Do You Do If They Ask about Price Right Away?

Once again, this is a problem you created yourself by talking about your offering too soon. At best, you can deflect the question by talking in generalities. For example, you might say, "Based on what we determine works best for your situation, it could range from nothing to $50,000. What we really need to do is analyze what's going on in your business in more depth." Then transition to a question focused on their business issues and challenges.

What Do You Do If You Walk in the Room and Six People Are Sitting There?

Unless you're really excellent at facilitating large meetings or engaging a group in a discussion without any preparation, you need to get out of this situation right away. Embarrassing as it may be, pull your contact aside for a talk. You might say something like this:

> "Teri, I appreciate that you've pulled together so many people who are interested in our offering. But I had no idea you were expecting a presentation today. And honestly, I think it's premature. Before I talk with your group, it's imperative for me to understand more about your critical marketing issues and what you've already done to tackle them.
>
> "I also typically meet with three to five different people in your organization—perhaps even some of the people sitting in that room—to get a better perspective of the challenge you're facing. At that point, I can pull together a very specific targeted presentation that addresses exactly what your group needs to know. My suggestion is that you and I spend an hour together today as planned and reschedule this meeting in a couple weeks."

Your contact may initially be a little shaken because he or she arranged the meeting. But this person would much rather have a good meeting with you than be embarrassed by your off-the-cuff presentation and so will nearly always agree. Believe it or not, most people in the room will be delighted to be excused as well because their desks are piled high with work. Also, because you've just discovered the high interest level in your offering, you may want to suggest individual meetings as your next follow-up step.

What Do You Do If You Catch Yourself Leaning Forward and Starting "The Pitch?"

Apologize to your prospects for getting carried away and talking about your offering. Tell them that much as you love your product, what's most important is to determine if it would provide business value to their organization. Then slowly lean back and ask another question.

As you can see, successful customer meetings don't just spontaneously occur on their own. They require the investment of a significant amount of time on the front end to ensure they're of high value to prospective customers.

If you've landed a meeting with a decision maker from a big company, you want it to go well. Take whatever time you need to fill out your Sales Call Planning Guide. The payback will be worth it.

KEY POINTS

- Sales to big companies take multiple calls. Plan your logical next step prior to each meeting. Know where you're going before you get there.
- Don't waste time on chitchat. Get down to business as quickly as possible. To increase your confidence, have your entire call mapped out before you meet with your prospective buyer.
- Focus on asking questions that explore their situation in more depth. Learn about their priorities and objectives as well as potential impediments to achieving them.
- Lean back when talking to corporate decision makers. This keeps you in a consultative mode and prevents you from pitching your product or service.
- At the end of your meeting, summarize your understanding of their situation and suggest the logical next step that advances the sales process.

22

THE MINDSET OF SUCCESS

In today's market, the hardest part of selling is getting that very first appointment with a corporate decision maker. As you well know, that's much easier said than done. At this point in the book, I'm sure that your head is reeling as you try to figure out how to integrate everything you've learned into your own account entry campaign.

Sometimes it can be overwhelming. So much to change, so little time. You may even be hitting yourself over the head for continuing with ineffective strategies for so long. Be gentle on yourself as you transition to this new methodology. It takes a while to really grasp how to think differently about your role as a seller, your offering, and your customer.

Anytime you learn something new, it's tough. When I was struggling to get back into big companies after my business crashed, I made lots of mistakes. Some were pretty embarrassing for someone who's a so-called "sales expert." There were times when, much to my chagrin, I had to literally pick myself up off the floor, dust myself off, and start over again. At one point, I was even fearful that I'd lost my touch and had nothing left to offer.

In order not to collapse under the weight of my own fears, I had to reframe the entire experience. Instead of considering myself a failure or a stupid idiot every time I screwed up, I decided to consider the experience a "valuable learning opportunity." For a while, it seemed like I was getting more than my fair share! But every single time I goofed or ran into a dead end, I challenged myself to find the lesson in the situation.

EXPERIMENT WITH SALES

As you proceed on this journey of rethinking your sales approach, I want to invite you to consider everything you're doing as a grand experiment. Don't wait until you think everything is perfect before you move ahead. You'll never make any progress that way.

Your job is to test things out. When you think you've articulated your value proposition pretty well, check it out with your colleagues, friends, or clients. If they clearly understand the difference you make for customers, you know you have made a good start. If not, go back to the drawing board again to figure out a new approach.

The same thing holds true when you think you've written a good sales letter or created an enticing voice mail message. Get other people's reactions. See if you can pass the instant delete test. If not, find out why. That's the only way you will improve.

When you consider everything you do as an experiment, you can't fail. Ever. I like that feeling. So will you. Plus, by considering all your prospect's reactions as simply data, it frees you to figure out what you might change to get a different reaction. Then you're on your way to finding out what will work.

Save Your Best Until Last

You now have a roadmap to follow that should guide you quite a distance in your quest to land large corporate clients. You're not going to be perfect at first. In fact, my guess is that you'll feel more than a bit awkward when you start using these new strategies and techniques.

So why in the world would you ever pursue business with your most desirable prospect when you're feeling your shakiest? Don't. It doesn't make any sense at all to put yourself under so much pressure when you're still trying to pull your whole approach together.

Call on your lower priority prospects instead. Perhaps these firms aren't ideal. Maybe they're not as prestigious. But they are safe places to practice—which is exactly what you need right now. Use these accounts to fine-tune your message. Work on crafting compelling voice mails, letters, or e-mails that elicit responses. Experiment with different questions when you're meeting with decision makers. Find out what it takes to keep the discussion focused on their business issues.

It takes a while to free yourself from old habits that no longer work with today's savvy corporate buyers. Rest assured, you'll get better over time. That's when you want to go after the really big, highly desirable companies that you'd drool to have as clients.

Keep On Learning

In sales, there is no perfection. There are only varying degrees of effectiveness. Sometimes what's effective for one person doesn't work at all with another, so you'll need more than one approach.

There are certainly more ways to get into big companies than have been described in this book. By all means, keep learning and growing. These methods work for me. I don't like a bunch of hype, gamesmanship, and manipulation. I prefer an approach that enables me to maintain my professional integrity at all times.

One thing I haven't touched on at all is how to attract clients to your business without making outbound calls. I'd strongly advise you to consider how you might leverage a variety of public relations strategies, speaking, writing, and the Internet to make this happen—especially if what you're selling is your expertise. These are long-term strategies that may take several years to deliver results, but they work incredibly well. However, when you need clients now, making sales calls is essential.

Finally, what do you do after the first meeting with a prospective client? As you advance the sales process, you'll need to develop other skills, such as proposal writing, presentations, or negotiation. There are tons of good resources on these subjects.

Use All the Resources at Your Disposal

You are not in this alone. If you're stuck, go talk to other people to get ideas. If you have colleagues, work on these challenges together. If you're a solo entrepreneur, form a group with others in similar positions.

Go talk to your customers too. Interview them. Learn from them. Ask them what it takes for a seller to get their attention. Tell them who your target market is, show them your scripts, letters, or questions, and get their reactions. Ask for brutal honesty and be prepared to listen. Never, ever defend what you've created if you want to hear the truth. Find out why they don't react positively. That's the jewel in the feedback, the seed for the changes that are needed.

HOLD YOURSELF ACCOUNTABLE

In order to be successful, it's absolutely imperative for you to assume total ownership of your success. If you blame others for your sales problems, you'll never make the changes necessary for you to be wildly successful.

It's not the fault of customers who just don't "get it." If they don't understand why they should make a change, ask yourself what you need to do to help them. If they can't see the difference between your offering and your competitors, figure out what you need to do to help them differentiate.

Nor does the problem rest with "rude" people who don't return phone calls. They're swamped; they don't have time to contact everyone who wants their attention. They may even be really nice people who feel terribly guilty about it. But modern technology has made abuses of time and etiquette more frequent, forcing many in the corporate world to erect barriers and filters.

The truth is, none of the problems you're running into are one bit personal. As a human being, you are not being rejected. Your prospective customers are only thinking about themselves and their own time. As soon as you tap into what they're interested in, the door opens for you.

Role-Play Even If You Hate It

Most everyone I know dislikes role-playing. But there's literally no better way to improve. Every time I try something new, my words trip all over each other as I struggle to pull them together into something coherent. Not only do my value propositions, questions, and success stories sound mangled at first, but I don't always focus on the most important points.

Unless you're some kind of sales savant, the likelihood that you can pull off an entirely new approach without practice is slim to none. So find someone to role-play with, even if you detest the thought. There's no other way to work out the bugs than by actually running through things in real time. That way you won't embarrass yourself when you're talking with a client— and you'll be much more effective.

Debrief after Every Call

Shortly after I was promoted into sales management, I attended a training session at our corporate headquarters. I still recall a key message that was shared with us. Only one in seven sales representatives fully debriefed after a client meeting—and the ones who did were the most successful sellers.

What exactly does it mean to *debrief*? After every interaction with a prospective client, ask yourself these questions:

- *What did I do well?* That's important to know so you can replicate it in future calls.
- *Where did I run into troubles or encounter resistance?* Try to find the root cause, the moment you started to get off track.
- *What can I change in the future?* The key is to come up with alternate ways to handle problem spots so they'll be eliminated in upcoming calls.

Effective selling is simply a skill. When you focus your attention on improving it, you get better. Only tackle one or two things at a time. Make sure you always debrief after sales calls. Even after all these years, I constantly assess and reassess what I'm doing. It's the only way to continually be your best.

REMEMBER WHAT'S IMPORTANT

We've covered a lot of ground in this book. In closing, I'd like to reiterate these key points, which can have a significant impact on your success in selling to big companies.

- Corporate decision makers are stretched to the limit these days. Time is their most precious commodity. They have no tolerance for anyone who might waste even a second of it.
- Prospective customers really don't care about your product, service, or solution. To them, it's simply a tool to solve their problems or achieve their business objectives.
- Focus on the difference you make, the results you deliver, and the outcomes customers can expect from working with your firm. That's all that's important.
- When pursuing large accounts, use a foot-in-the-door strategy. Figure out how to get a "toe-hold" project or order in one area and deliver impressive results before expanding to other parts of the company.
- Plan an account entry campaign from the very start. Expect to make multiple contacts before you get an appointment. Use a variety of mediums such as voice mail, e-mail, direct mail, and faxes.
- Invest time preparing for every customer contact. Research their business and personalize your approach. That's how you can differentiate yourself from all the other sellers vying for the prospect's time.
- When you meet with a corporate decision maker, have a conversation focused on the business issues that you can impact. Before you go in, know your logical next step and plan your questions.

Finally, realize that *you* are the biggest differentiator of all. Become an expert. Know your customer's business, processes, and marketplace trends as well as they do. Deepen your knowledge of your product line, capabilities, and total solution capacity.

Constantly be thinking about how you can help your customers improve their operations and reach their goals. Competitors can create copycat products and services overnight, but no one can replicate you and your brain. Your ability to provide a continuous stream of fresh ideas, insights, and information to corporate buyers will make you irresistible, invaluable, and, ultimately, indispensable.

KEY POINTS

- Experiment with sales. There is no right or wrong way—only some ways that are more effective. Continually test your approaches, evaluate what worked, and try again.
- Practice on your low priority prospects before you tackle your top priorities. Give yourself a chance to develop your confidence first.
- Focus on lifelong learning. If you do, you'll be ahead of 95 percent of the sellers out there. Develop your expertise in all the areas that surround your offering.
- Ask for help. There's no reason you have to go it alone. Engage others in figuring out what works. Learn from the pros; tap into their knowledge.
- Remember, *you are the key!* Ultimately it's you who makes the difference, not your offering. Work on becoming the differentiator.

ACCOUNT ENTRY TOOL KIT

TOOL 1: TARGET MARKET DEFINITION

TOOL 2: PAST CUSTOMER ANALYSIS

TOOL 3: OFFERING ASSESSMENT

TOOL 4: PERSONAL CREDIBILITY APPRAISAL

TOOL 5: CLARIFYING YOUR VALUE PROPOSITION

TOOL 6: TOP TEN TARGETED ACCOUNTS

TOOL 7: VOICE MAIL SCRIPT TEMPLATE

TOOL 8: THE VOICE MAIL EVALUATOR

TOOL 9: SALES CALL PLANNING GUIDE

TOOL I
TARGET MARKET DEFINITION

The ability to clearly define your target market significantly impacts your sales success. In the space provided describe the characteristics of an ideal client for your company.

1. Demographics *(the basic facts)*

2. Psychographics *(the "fit" factors)*

3. Enabling Conditions *(challenges, issues, problems; goals, objectives, strategic imperatives)*

TOOL 2
PAST CUSTOMER ANALYSIS

If you've been in business for a while, you probably already have developed some expertise in a particular market niche, but you may still be keeping multiple options open. Below are questions you can ask to determine if some fine tuning is needed. Consider demographic and psychographic factors as well as enabling conditions. Be as specific as you can.

1. What type of businesses have you been most successful with in the past?

2. What type of companies have you struggled with or want to avoid in the future? What do they have in common?

3. What types of customers have been the most profitable? Enjoyable? What are their characteristics?

4. Have you noticed any particular conditions that trigger more need for your offering?

TOOL 3
OFFERING ASSESSMENT

Another way to determine your best target market is to work backwards from your offering. This can help you figure out what types of companies would receive the most value from your products, services, or solutions.

1. What are the primary benefits of your offering?

2. If an organization is not using your products, services, or solutions, what problems are they likely encountering?

3. If an organization doesn't use your offering, what opportunities might they be missing out on?

4. List the characteristics of those companies whose current situation could be dramatically improved by your products or services.

TOOL 4
PERSONAL CREDIBILITY APPRAISAL

Often, when you're just starting out—especially as an independent service provider—you may not be sure what your offering is or which customers might benefit most from what you do. Use the following questions to stimulate thinking about your ideal target market:

1. What specific expertise do I have? What am I really good at? What do I do so effortlessly that I don't even realize it's a "big deal"?

2. When I worked inside a company what problems did I solve for my employer? What were the business ramifications of these problems?

3. How would I describe the demographics, psychographics, and enabling conditions of the last organization in which I made an impact?

Note: When you're an independent professional, you have the highest credibility with companies similar to your past employers. It's much easier to build a business in your area of strength than to start fresh in an area where you have not demonstrated any success.

TOOL 5
CLARIFYING YOUR VALUE PROPOSITION

Understanding how your customer benefits from using your product or service is essential in clarifying your value proposition. Use this worksheet to determine the value of your offering.

1. Establish the customer's current situation. *Without your product or service, how do your prospective customers do things today?*

2. Define the problem or gaps with their current solution. *What problems does your offering solve? What opportunities does it create?*

3. Clarify the business implications. *Explore the "ripple effect." Find other areas in their company that are impacted by the above problems or gaps.*

4. Determine the value of making a change. *What's the payoff from using your product, service, or solution? Tangible value? Intangible value? Opportunity costs?*

TOOL 6
TOP TEN TARGETED ACCOUNTS

In the space below, list the ten big companies that you'll be pursuing business with in the upcoming year. Make sure you break the account down into an opportunity you can get your arms around.

Company Name	Business Unit or Division	Department or Functional Area
1.		
2.		
3.		
4.		
5.		
6.		
7.		
8.		
9.		
10.		

TOOL 7
VOICE MAIL SCRIPT TEMPLATE

Use the following template as a guideline to prepare scripts for the personalized voice mails you can use to contact big companies:

1. Establish credibility. *Reference your referral, the research you conducted, or a triggering event.*

2. Pique curiosity. *Communicate your value proposition, share an insightful idea, or dangle important information.*

3. Close confidently.

TOOL 8
THE VOICE MAIL EVALUATOR

Call several of your colleagues and leave your message on their voice mail. To get the honest feedback you need to craft a customer-enticing message, ask them to complete this assessment after listening to it.

1. Would you have deleted this voice mail at any point prior to the end? If so, when?

2. Check everything that bothered you about this voice mail:

   _____ Could tell it was a salesperson immediately.

   _____ Told me about their company and how wonderful it was.

   _____ Tried to convince me their offering was something I should buy.

   _____ Included "cute" slogans about their company.

   _____ Sounded like they were reading a script.

   _____ Used words and phrases to sound important.

   _____ Used company jargon or acronyms.

   _____ Tried to "close" me like old-time salesperson.

   _____ Sounded scared or subservient to the decision maker.

   _____ Pronounced my name incorrectly.

   _____ Spoke too fast; hard to understand message.

   _____ Sounded unsure of their ability to add value.

   _____ Felt like I was being sold.

   _____ Nonpersonalized to my situation.

   _____ Babbled on and on. Never seemed to get to the point.

3. Other feedback?

TOOL 9
SALES CALL PLANNING GUIDE

Use this tool to plan your first meeting with a corporate decision maker. Make sure you're prepared.

State your desired logical next step: _____

_____

I. Open the Conversation. (5–10 minutes)

A.   Make the introductions.

B.   Confirm times and agenda.

II. Lead the Discussion. (40–45 minutes)

A.   Set the stage. (5 minutes)
Share your value proposition, customer success scenarios, ideas you've developed, or important information you're bringing.

B.   Transition to questions: What will you say to transition?

C.   Focus on business issues. (35–40 minutes)
      List your Top Ten questions below.

    1.

    2.

    3.

    4.

    5.

    6.

    7.

    8.

    9.

    10.

III. Advance the Process. (5–10 minutes)

A.   Summarize your understanding.

B.   Suggest the logical next step.

RECOMMENDED RESOURCES

Online Business Research

Big Charts *http://www.bigcharts.com*
Biz Stats *http://www.bizstats.com*
Business Journals *http://www.bizjournals.com*
Company Financials *http://www.companyfinancials.com*
Corporate Information *http://www.corporateinformation.com*
Edgar Scan *http://www.edgarscan.pwcglobal.com*
Find Articles *http://www.findarticles.com*
Glossarist *http://www.glossarist.com/glossaries/business*
Google News *http://news.google.com*
Hoovers *http://www.hoovers.com*
James J. Hill Reference Library *http://www.hillsearch.org*
Newslink *http://www.newslink.org*
Technorati *http://www.technorati.com*
The Wayback Machine *http://www.waybackmachine.org*
Thomas Register *http://www.thomasregister.com*
Yahoo! News *http://news.yahoo.com*

Online Communities and Contact Locators

Jigsaw *http://www.jigsaw.com*
Spoke *http://www.spoke.com*
LinkedIn *http://www.linkedin.com*
Ryze *http://www.ryze.com*
Ecademy *http://www.ecademy.com/*
Contact Network *http://www.contactnetworkcorp.com*
Tacit *http://www.tacit.com*
Visible Path *http://www.visiblepath.com*
InterAction *http://www.interaction.com*

Select Minds *http://www.selectminds.com*
Leverage Software *http://www.leveragesoftware.com*
Zero Degrees *http://www.zerodegrees.com*

Reading Material

The following books are excellent resources and complement the sales strategies in *Selling to Big Companies*.

Guerilla Marketing for Consultants, Jay Levinson and Mike McLaughlin, John Wiley, 2004
The Little Red Book of Selling, Jeffrey Gitomer, Bard Press, 2004
ROI Selling, Michael Nick and Kurt Koenig, Dearborn Trade, 2004
Cold Calling for Women, Wendy Weiss, DFD Publications, 2000
How Winners Sell, Dave Stein, Dearborn Trade, 2004
Secrets of Question Based Selling, Thomas Freese, Sourcebooks, 2000
Selling to VITO, Anthony Parinello, Adams Media, 1999
SPIN Selling, Neil Rackham, McGraw-Hill, 1988
Major Account Sales Strategies, Neil Rackham, McGraw-Hill, 1989
Think Like Your Customer, Bill Stinnett, McGraw-Hill, 2004
Mastering the Complex Sale, Jeff Thull, John Wiley, 2003
Beyond Selling Value, Mark Shonka and Dan Kosch, Dearborn Trade, 2002
Team Selling, Steve Waterhouse, McGraw-Hill, 2003
Customer Centric Selling, Michael Bosworth and John Holland, McGraw-Hill, 2003
Selling the Invisible, Harry Beckwith, Warner Business Books, 1997

ABOUT THE AUTHOR

Jill Konrath is a recognized expert on selling to large corporations. She helps sellers shorten their sales cycle, increase their account penetration rate, and win more contracts in the highly competitive business-to-business marketplace.

Even more importantly, Konrath helps her clients develop new ways to create significant value for their customers—a distinctive and powerful competitive advantage.

Most recently Konrath has been featured in *Selling Power, Entrepreneur, The Business Journal, Sales & Marketing Management, WSJ's Start-Up Journal, Sales & Marketing Excellence, Journal of Marketing, Business Advisor,* and countless online publications. She's been interviewed by Sales Rep Radio, Entrepreneur Radio, and many local stations.

With names like 3M, Medtronic, United HealthGroup, General Mills, RSM McGladrey, and Hilton, Konrath's client list reflects some of the world's leading sales organizations. In recent years she has leveraged technology to make her expertise available to smaller companies, professional services firms and independent professionals.

For more information on training programs, workshops or speaking engagements, please contact us at:

Jill Konrath
CEO & Chief Sales Officer
Selling to Big Companies
2227 Foxtail Ct.
White Bear Lake, MN 55110
Office: (651) 429-1922 Fax: (651) 426-0983
E-mail: jill@sellingtobigcompanies.com
Web site: http://www.sellingtobigcompanies.com
Blog: http://sellingtobigcompanies.blogs.com